Umbrella Guide to

Grand Old Hotels
of Washington and Oregon

by
Christine Ummel

UMBRELLA
BOOKS ®

An imprint of Epicenter Press

Editor: Kent Sturgis
Cover design: Elizabeth Watson
Cover photo: Courtesy of the Majestic Hotel, Anacortes, Wash.
Maps: Scott Penwell
Pre-press production: Newman Design/Illustration
Printer: McNaughton & Gunn

© 1994 Christine Ummel
ISBN 0-945397-26-7
Library of Congress Catalog Card Number: 94-94291

To order single copies of UMBRELLA GUIDE TO GRAND OLD HOTELS OF WASHINGTON AND OREGON, mail $12.95 (Washington residents add $1.06 state sales tax) plus $2 for shipping and handling to: Epicenter Press, Box 82368, Kenmore Station, Seattle, WA 98028. BOOKSELLERS: Retail discounts are available from our trade distributor, Graphic Arts Center Publishing Co., Portland, OR, phone 800-452-3032.

PRINTED IN THE UNITED STATES OF AMERICA
First printing, June 1994
10 9 8 7 6 5 4 3 2 1

Acknowledgements

Many people have been extremely kind and patient in assisting me in my research for this book, especially the management of the hotels described within. My sincere thanks also to the Seattle Public Library, the King County Library System, the Multnomah County Library, the Oregon Historical Society, the Southern Oregon Historical Society, the San Juan Historical Society, the Jefferson County Historical Society, Joyce Webb in Port Townsend, the Island County Historical Society, the Hood River Historical Society, the Ilwaco Heritage Museum, Bill Dengler at Mt. Rainier National Park, the Anacortes Historical Society, the Anacortes Public Library, the Newport Historical Society, Kerin Covall at the Hoquiam Castle, Patricia Swenson at KBPS-AM in Portland, Linny Adamson at the Timberline Lodge, the Astoria Public Library, the Clallam County Historical Society, and the Olympic National Park headquarters in Port Angeles. A special word of thanks to Kevin Richardson at the Oregon Caves Chateau, who believed me when I said I was writing a book, and to the incredibly patient librarians at the Port Angeles Public Library, who were still helping me twenty minutes after closing time.

For giving me the truly remarkable opportunity to write this book, I would like to thank my editor Kent Sturgis and God (do I need to reverse that order?). Many thanks to all the wonderful teachers and professors who over the years have encouraged my writing and, more importantly, criticized it. My eternal gratitude to the loyal friends, particularly Katrina Miller and Jenny Chen, whose laughter and friendship helped keep me sane while I was trying to get this book written. Finally, all my love to my dear family, without whose support, both financial and emotional, this book would not have been possible.

Table of Contents

Introduction

When I began work on this project, I naively assumed that I would be able to describe all (or at least most) of the historic hotels in Washington and Oregon.

Wrong.

I was amazed to discover that, when I added up all the historic hotels, lodges, inns, and bed-and-breakfasts, I had counted about 400 in these two states alone. With so many wonderful places to choose from, my editor Kent Sturgis and I decided to cover only the best of the best. I would look for about thirty of the most spectacular, most unusual, and most enjoyable historic hotels in the Northwest, and discuss them in all the detail they deserved.

Here's the criteria I used to select the hotels:

- I wanted to include buildings that were not just old, but historically significant (or at least historically interesting). The hotels described here represent a variety of phases in Northwest history: the stage coach days of the 1870s; the boom town blitzes of the 1880s; the Victorian gentility of the 1890s; the optimistic extravagance of the 1920s; even the desperate hopes of the Great Depression. You'll find that most of these buildings are at least seventy-five years old. Most are listed on the National Register of Historic Places. All have fascinating stories to tell.

- I looked for a variety of architectural styles and features. For example, I didn't want them all to be downtown high-rise hotels or all Queen Anne Victorian mansions.

- I selected hotels in locations where people would want to spend time anyway. Some are in big cities, or on the shores of the ocean, or high in the mountains. Others are in towns that are interesting to visit for historic reasons — not "theme towns" that have been built to attract tourists, but real historic districts such as the ghost town of Shaniko or the gold rush town of Jacksonville. A few are found off the beaten track, in tiny hamlets surrounded by wilderness where the only thing to do is relax.

- Also, I tried to find places that most people could afford to visit in one way or another. I looked for a wide range of room rates, so they wouldn't all be beyond someone's budget. Besides, someone who can't afford a room in one of these fine establishments might still enjoy eating dinner there or even just catching a peek of the lobby.

I hope you'll agree that these are not your standard motels by the side of the road. They have more class, more atmosphere.

They also have more restrictions. In some, smoking is not allowed, either because it would be a fire hazard in such an old building or because the management wants to maintain a clean atmosphere. Children are discouraged in some hotels, often because noise travels too easily through thin walls built before the invention of soundproofing. Pets are usually prohibited, with a few exceptions. I've listed all the main restrictions with each hotel, but it's a good idea to call them with any extra questions you might have, just in case.

Also, not all these historic hotels have the modern-day conveniences that many of today's tourists expect. In some guest rooms, you won't find television sets, telephones, or even private bathrooms. For some people, this may be a problem. For others, it will be a blessing.

And, of course, these hotels will be more expensive than the average motel. Please note that the room rates listed are intended to give you an idea of the price range. They are current at the time of this printing — the spring of 1994 — but are subject to change and undoubtedly will increase as time goes on.

One more thing sets these hotels apart: the ghost stories.

Personally, I am not a great believer in ghosts, and I didn't expect to put any spook stories in this book. Yet as I visited each hotel on my list, I was amazed at the number of ghost stories that people eagerly told me. It seemed unfair to leave them all out, but it would have been monotonous to put them all in. So I've included a few of my favorites, just for fun. I hope that no prospective visitors will be scared away by these stories — the proprietors of these hotels all emphasized that they were haunted only by benevolent or harmless spirits. Anyway, my wish is that these stories will make your stay just a bit more of an adventure.

Happy traveling.

Christine Ummel

Washington

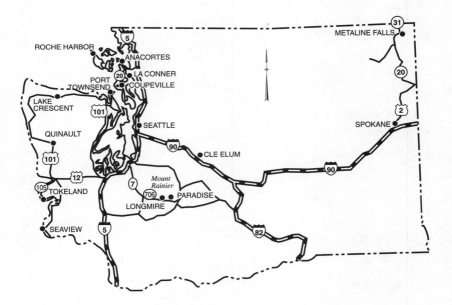

The fanciful Hotel de Haro was once at the center of an industrial company town, ruled by lime manufacturer John Stafford McMillin.

Hotel de Haro

Roche Harbor Resort and Marina
P.O. Box 4001
Roche Harbor, WA 98250
(206) 378-2155 / (800) 451-8910

History

Some called him a tyrant. Others described him as a respected business leader. But no one questioned that John Stafford McMillin was king of Roche Harbor.

McMillin originally was trained as a lawyer in his home state of Indiana. After bringing his family to Tacoma, Washington in 1884, he turned from practicing law to the more profitable lime business. Formed by "burning" limestone in a kiln, this powder was a main ingredient in steel, plaster, and cement — vital building materials in the growing cities of the West Coast.

Large, rich deposits of lime had been discovered on San Juan Island during the notorious "Pig War," when British and American troops were stationed there for twelve uneventful years while their respective governments bickered over who owned the islands. Some British officers kept their men busy quarrying and burning limestone at the north end of the island. When a neutral arbitrator, Germany's Kaiser Wilhelm I, awarded the islands to the United States in 1872 and the English had to withdraw, brothers Robert and Richard Scurr set up a small lime operation in their place. In 1886 McMillin bought the property and began building an empire.

By 1890, McMillin had set up a full-scale corporation at Roche Harbor. Limestone was dug out of McMillin's quarries, burned in his twelve steel kilns, packed into barrels made by his factory, and sent out on ships in his fleet. In thirty years, the Tacoma and Roche Harbor Lime Co. would be producing 1,500 barrels of lime per day, making it the largest producer west of the Mississippi.

Roche Harbor was a company town. Employees lived on company land, single men in bunkhouses, families in cottages. Much of their wages was paid in "scrip" — coupons redeemable only at the company store. McMillin tried to influence the way his men voted and to discourage them from forming unions; when one group of workers went on strike, McMillin solved the problem by firing everyone involved, some fifty men. Company foremen carried handguns and locked employees out of the town if they misbehaved. Life at Roche Harbor wasn't all bad, however. McMillin provided workers with their own resident doctor, a post office, a school for their children, and a barber who visited twice a month. Picnics and dances were held for their entertainment.

Usually, though, McMillin concentrated on more important guests: governors, foreign dignitaries, wealthy businessmen interested in purchasing lime. The visitors stayed at the Hotel de Haro, constructed in 1887 around a log bunkhouse the Scurr brothers had built in 1881. (In an archway on the second floor, you can see the wood beams of the bunkhouse inside the hotel walls.) The ornate, white-painted hotel had twenty-two rooms, a triple balcony, and a decorative cupola. During his guests' stay, McMillin would treat them to outdoor salmon barbecues, fashion shows, Christmas dinners, dances on floating barges, and cruises on his fifty-foot yacht.

McMillin's most honored guest was Theodore Roosevelt. The president came in 1906 and again in 1907, probably to thank McMillin for his life-long support of the Republican Party; McMillin was so influential that he was almost elected U.S. senator. (Today you can stay in Room 2B, where Roosevelt stayed, and sleep in the wooden sleigh bed that he used. A portrait of the president hangs over the staircase, and the lobby hotel register displays his signature.)

In spite of McMillin's wealth, power, and influential friends, his reign didn't last forever. In 1922, McMillin's oldest son, whom he had groomed to take over for him, died at age forty-two. Just one year later, a fire destroyed the lime plant, the barrel factory, the offices, and the warehouse

4

dock — everything had to be rebuilt. McMillin lost hope in the future of the company and began to focus instead on constructing an elaborate family mausoleum. After McMillin's own death in 1936, his younger son Paul had difficulty running the business. The quarries were running out of lime, and much of the old equipment was breaking down.

Paul McMillin sold Roche Harbor to Reuben Tarte, a Seattle business-man, in 1956. The Tarte family gradually transformed the company town into an island resort, turning the McMillin family home into a fine restau-rant, the workers' housing into vacation cottages, and the tiny schoolhouse into a Catholic chapel. The family brought back to life the estate's formal gardens and the long-unused Hotel de Haro; they built a 200-boat marina and an Olympic-size swimming pool. Though no longer owned by the Tarte family, the picture-perfect resort, with its green trim and white picket fences, is now a favorite destination for boaters and vacationers from all over the Northwest.

The Hotel de Haro today

Unlike most historic buildings, the Hotel de Haro never has undergone major renovation — you can see it in the warped floors and slanting walls. The modest, tasteful rooms are decorated almost entirely in antiques, many from John McMillin's time. Few of the rooms have private baths; guests wanting to bathe sometimes line up in the hall. For women, though, it may be worth the wait for a turn to use the huge wood-rimmed bathtub up on claw feet in the second-floor ladies room.

The hotel's lobby, though decorated with interesting artifacts from the resort's past, is hardly a comfortable place to pass the time. You'll prefer sitting in a wicker chair out on the ivy-covered balcony. When you get hungry, head across the street to the posh, popular restaurant. Its elaborate dinners, like garlic prawns and rock salt-roasted prime rib, cost $15-20.

What to do around Roche Harbor

First, buy a copy of **"A Walking Tour of Historic Roche Harbor"** in the hotel lobby. This booklet will take you not only to the kilns and quarries of McMillin's empire, but also on a short walk to see the McMillin family **mausoleum**, a complex stone monument filled with symbolism from Masonry, the Bible, and Sigma Chi fraternity. At Roche Harbor resort, you can enjoy a heated **swimming pool, tennis courts**, and **volleyball nets**, or rent a **canoe** or **paddleboat** to explore the harbor. Elsewhere on the island, you can visit the restored **American Camp** and **English Camp** to learn about the history of the Pig War. In the island's main town, **Friday Harbor**, you'll find shops, restaurants, art galleries, and the San Juan Historical Museum. **Other islands** in the San Juans can be visited by ferry boat.

Room Rates: Rooms $45-60, suites with bath $65-100, cottages $93-103.

Reservations: May be necessary eight to ten months in advance for July and August, for special occasions like the Fourth of July, or for suites.

Restrictions: Pets not allowed, smoking discouraged.

Room Features: Telephones, few private baths, no television sets.

How to get there

Take the ferry from Anacortes to San Juan Island. When the ferry arrives at Friday Harbor, drive on Spring Street from the dock, then turn right onto Second Avenue. Take a right onto Tucker Avenue, which will become Roche Harbor Road. Follow it north to Roche Harbor.

The Majestic Hotel has seen many occupants and several locations in its long, complicated lifetime.

Majestic Hotel

419 Commercial Avenue
Anacortes, WA 98221
(206) 293-3355

History

It was built on the west end of town, but it didn't stay there for long.

The highly mobile McNaught Building was constructed during Anacortes' boom years. Like many small Puget Sound towns during the 1880s, Anacortes had dreams of greatness. Rumor had it that the first transcontinental railroad was coming to Fidalgo Island, and would make Anacortes the "New York of the West." Thousands of investors came to buy land in the "Magic City." The trouble was that no one knew exactly where this metropolis would be, so no one knew where its downtown would be. As a result, people bought any land they could get their hands on, hoping it would turn out to be valuable downtown property. Land the government had practically given away for $2-10 per acre in 1886 was being sold for as much as $1,000 per acre in 1890.

Real estate speculators were going crazy, including James McNaught. As a consultant for the Northern Pacific Railroad, McNaught thought he was getting valuable inside information about the coming of the railroad. McNaught placed his bets on the west side of town, where he bought property and built a wharf, a storehouse, offices, stores, and a hotel.

At the heart of the "McNaught Addition" was the "McNaught Building." Constructed in 1890, this wood frame building was square with a roof shaped like a pyramid, and was designed in the upscale French Colonial style. The building soon was filled with shops and offices, particularly the

9

headquarters of McNaught's real estate business; the upper levels may have been used as hotel rooms. At its peak, the McNaught Building bustled with busy doctors, lawyers, architects, and real estate men.

Not long afterward, however, Anacortes' boom years came to an abrupt end. Late in 1890, the news reached town that the railroads weren't coming. Many investors were ruined as the land they had paid thousands of dollars for suddenly became virtually worthless. McNaught was hit especially hard. Not only was his development not in the middle of a big city, it wasn't even in the middle of a small town. Anacortes' downtown, such as it was, had grown up on the opposite side of town. McNaught managed to hold on to his office building until 1907, but by then it was practically empty.

The building's new owner, R. Lee Bradley, wanted to use it for his store, the Anacortes Mercantile Co. Bradley had the building lifted off its foundation and set onto a row of logs. As a crowd of cheering spectators looked on, the building was hooked to a team of horses and pulled half a mile across town, to a spot in downtown Anacortes.

Even this new location wasn't permanent. For reasons unclear, the building had been set down in the middle of Fifth Street. (It's possible that a new street system was laid down, and the building's location suddenly became a problem). A year and a half later, the building had to be picked up and moved again.

As the home of the Anacortes Mercantile Co., the building was the largest store in Skagit County, where townspeople could buy fashionable clothing and fabric. From the Depression into the early 1960s, it was used as Allen's Grocery and Meat Market. Sadly, as the building grew older, it also deteriorated. It was used as a second-hand store, then as storage space.

After standing empty for several years, the McNaught Building was purchased in 1984 by developer Richard Ballow, who renovated it to make a hotel called the White Gull Inn. Both the exterior and the interior were stripped away, leaving only the framework intact. Once again, the building was moved — this time five feet straight up, to make room for a new floor and a new foundation. Ballow's efforts were plagued by financial problems, however, and he went bankrupt in 1988.

The building's new owners, Virginia and Jeff Wetmore, completed the renovation. The finished hotel had four floors of guest rooms, with a wooden staircase winding through the center up to a decorative lookout tower. Virginia Wetmore, an interior designer by trade, decorated each of the twenty-three rooms herself, and filled them with fine European antiques that she and her husband had collected during their travels around the world. The new Majestic Hotel opened in June of 1990.

The Majestic Hotel today

In spite of its unique past and gorgeous antique furnishings, the Majestic has a surprisingly modern feel. Its interior flows in delicious curves: high arched windows, round balconies, rippling staircases. Eclectic guest rooms display contemporary shapes and designer color schemes. One suite is thoroughly Asian, exotically decorated in black, gold, and deep red, with lacquered Chinese furnishings. Most rooms, however, are more European, trimmed in rich colors with wicker furniture, ceiling fans, and cast iron radiators. The fanciest rooms include such features as marble bathrooms with oversized soaking tubs, wet bars, refrigerators, and private sun decks.

Guests in the Majestic Hotel have a variety of interesting public rooms to explore. Besides the elegant two-story lobby, there's a British-style library, paneled in mahogany, and an English country garden out back. A roof-top cupola offers a 360-degree view of Anacortes, Mt. Baker, and the San Juan Islands. Downstairs, gourmet Northwest seafood is served in the "Courtyard Bistro," a formal dining room with a sophisticated French decor (dinners $15-22). A rowdier atmosphere can be found at the London-style "Rose & Crown Pub," which has as its centerpiece a white marble bar taken from a pharmacy soda fountain.

What to do in Anacortes

The Majestic sits in the middle of **downtown Anacortes**, where you'll find turn-of-the-century buildings and murals showing scenes from the town's early days. Five major marinas make the town a popular place for **boating**. Locals enjoy hiking up **Mt. Erie** and watching romantic sunsets from atop **Cap Sante Peak**. Fidalgo Island is filled with parks, a favorite being **Deception Pass State Park**, where you can go camping or picnicking. Because it's so close to the ferry terminal, many people use Anacortes as a starting place for trips into the **San Juan Islands**.

11

Room Rates: Rooms $89-138, suites $177.

Reservations: Not always necessary during the week, recommended two to three weeks in advance for most summer weekends.

Restrictions: No pets, no smoking except in the pub and in specified smoking rooms.

Room Features: Television sets with cable, telephones, private baths, coffee machines, down comforters.

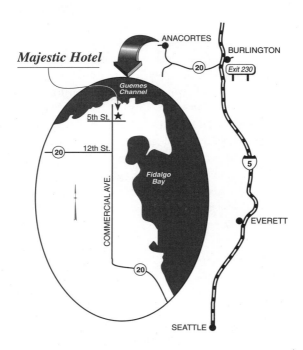

How to get there

From Interstate 5, take Exit 230 in Burlington and head west on Highway 20 for seventeen miles until you reach Anacortes. There, Highway 20 becomes Commercial Avenue. The hotel will be on your right, on the corner of Fifth Street and Commercial.

Hotel Planter

715 First Street
La Conner, WA 98257
(206) 466-4710

History

La Conner is an artist's dream.

A slow, silvery channel of water wanders past the sleepy town. Sunsets streak the surface with brillant colors. Nearby, gentle breezes brush over low fields of farmland. The beauty of the Skagit Valley has inspired artists for decades, and, in turn, artists have shaped the destiny of La Conner.

It didn't start out that way, of course. Founded in 1864, it was the first town in Skagit County. One of its pioneers, John Conner, concocted the town's name out of the initials of his wife, Louisa A. Conner. Built on the banks of the Swinomish Channel, La Conner started out as a small fishing village. As time passed, it became the hub of trade between farmers in the fertile Skagit Valley and steamships coming up from Seattle with passengers and freight.

By 1900, the town's population exceeded 1,000. Hotels and restaurants went up rapidly. In 1907, a new hotel was built in the ultra-modern Chicago style. It was made of solid concrete blocks, ten inches thick. The blocks were made on location from molds ordered from the Sears, Roebuck Co., and the building took a while to complete because the workers had to make concrete blocks, one at a time, as they went along.

The "Hotel Planter" was worth the wait, apparently. It featured all the latest conveniences, such as electricity and a cement sidewalk out front. The L-shaped, two-story hotel even had indoor plumbing — one bathroom

At the turn of the century, the Hotel Planter was constructed in the ultra-modern Chicago style, out of solid concrete blocks.

among twenty-two guest rooms. Throughout the 1910s and 1920s, the Hotel Planter was a profitable, reputable establishment, housing young fishermen and cannery workers who ate their meals in the dining room on the first floor. Wealthy tourists also stayed there occasionally, sailing in from Seattle or Everett on board one of the ships of the Mosquito Fleet to enjoy a quiet holiday hunting birds or fishing for salmon.

Then the Depression came. La Conner was hit hard. The fishing industry went into decline. All the town's young men left to find jobs elsewhere. It was during the Depression that poor artists began to discover La Conner, a quiet, picturesque town in a spectacular natural setting where you could live dirt cheap.

By the 1950s, a community of broke Beatnik artists and writers had taken over La Conner, and the center of that community was the Hotel Planter. Many artists lived in the tiny, cheap rooms, or (if they couldn't afford a room) slept out in the hall. The hotel's residents, doing odd jobs or carpentry work to pay the rent, often lived on one meal a day, sent up from the restaurant downstairs. The cold, concrete building was heated by one wood stove in the hallway; to warm up their rooms, residents opened the transom windows above their doors to let the heat in. The only safety features in the crowded hotel were pieces of rope, bolted to the floor, that could be tossed out the window and used as fire escapes in the event of an emergency.

Change came again during the 1960s, when La Conner's artists started being discovered by the art world. The work of many, like painter Guy Anderson and sculptor Clayton James, gained national acclaim. The region itself started getting attention, and today La Conner is a popular destination for tourists.

In the rush for prosperity, however, the dilapidated Hotel Planter was left behind. Even into the early 1980s, it housed mostly factory workers and starving artists. By 1986, the hotel had closed, become an eyesore, and was condemned. Enter Don Hoskins. A junior high school art teacher who made pottery on the side, Hoskins had started his own gallery, called "Earthenworks." When Hoskins wanted to move his gallery to La Conner, he found that the only vacant building in town large enough was the Hotel Planter. So Hoskins and his wife rented space on the first floor to house the gallery.

After seven years of renting, the Hoskins decided to buy the building and turn the second floor back into a hotel. It took over two years and a half million dollars. They added skylights and private bathrooms, consolidating the original twenty-two rooms into twelve larger ones. The Hoskins salvaged all they could from the old hotel, re-using the original doors, windows, railings, and wood trim. Re-opened in 1989, the Hotel Planter is now the only historic hotel in the historic district of La Conner.

The Hotel Planter today

The "new" Hotel Planter strives to combine the style of the 1910s with the modern comforts of the 1990s. The rooms are small, but the eleven-foot-high ceilings and long windows make them feel bright and airy. All of the rooms look about the same, except for one deluxe room that has a jacuzzi bathtub. The wood furniture was custom-made to have an old-fashioned look. Other classy furnishings include wicker chairs and spinning ceiling fans. The bathrooms, with their tile floors and podium sinks, also have an antiquated feel.

The hotel isn't designed to be a place to pass the time — there's no restaurant, no lounge. Though attractive, the lobby is a place to check in, not to relax. Your only retreat is the

COURTESY OF THE HOTEL PLANTER

Now tastefully decorated, the halls of this hotel were home to a community of Beatnik artists in the 1950s.

quiet garden out back, where you can linger at an umbrella table on the patio or soak away your troubles in the big, gazebo-covered hot tub.

What to do in La Conner

This little wharf town now overflows with clothing boutiques, antique shops, and restaurants. Many local artists have galleries here (although, ironically, few undiscovered artists can afford to live in trendy La Conner these days). Other artists display their work at the **Valley Museum of Northwestern Art**, housed in the Victorian **Gaches Mansion**. The **Skagit County Historical Museum** displays artifacts from the valley's pioneer days, while the **La Conner Volunteer Fireman's Museum** shows off firefighting equipment from 1884. Skagit Valley's most popular attraction is its magnificent **tulips fields**, in bloom every spring.

Room Rates: Regular rooms $70-90, suite with Jacuzzi $110.

Restrictions: No smoking, no pets, children discouraged.

Reservations: Thirty days in spring and summer, two months for the Tulip Festival.

Room Features: Private bathrooms, television sets, telephones.

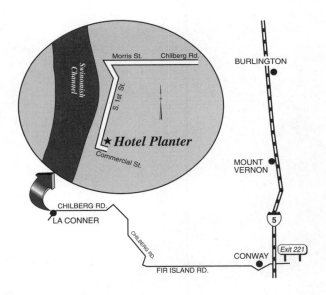

How to get there
From Interstate 5, take Exit 221 south of Mount Vernon. Go west on Fir Island Road, which becomes first Chilberg Road, then Morris Street. At the end of the road, turn left onto South First Street and continue through town until you see the Hotel Planter on your left; it's on the corner of First and Commercial.

Built out of peeled madrona logs in 1907, this log cabin-like inn was part of Judge Lester Still's popular Whidbey Island resort.

Captain Whidbey Inn

2072 W Captain Whidbey Inn Road
Coupeville, WA 98239
(800) 366-4097

History

For more than 200 years, people have judged this quiet, protected cove to be a special place.

In 1792, ships under the command of British captain George Vancouver brought the first European sailors to this long, thin island in Puget Sound. Taking the word of Joseph Whidbey, who had explored the area and said this cove was one of the finest he had ever seen, Vancouver named the bay "Penn's Cove," according to his journals, "in honour of a particular friend."

More than sixty years later, sometime around 1854, the first trading post on Whidbey Island was established on Penn's Cove. Owned by Captain Benjamin Barstow, the trading post offered early settlers everything from smoking tobacco and bars of soap to chickens and pigs.

After Barstow's death, the trading post closed. The land was eventually sold to Lester Still, a young lawyer working in nearby Coupeville. Still's spotless record as a prosecuting attorney earned him such respect that he was appointed Supreme Court Judge of Island County in 1907, at age thirty-five. Though life was usually quiet on the island, Judge Still did try some interesting cases. One woman called "Dr. Hazard," a diet consultant for young ladies, was brought to trial after one of her patients starved to death.

As Still's legal career progressed, so did his work on another project: turning his 160 acres of land on Penn's Cove into a summer resort. In 1907,

Still hired Peter and Christopher Solid to construct an inn (making it, as the current owners like to say, "a solidly built inn"). They built the inn by hand, primarily out of peeled madrona logs, giving it the rustic appearance of a huge log cabin. The "Whid-Isle Inn" had fourteen guest rooms, a two-story verandah, two massive fireplaces, and a large dining room, but no indoor plumbing. The only "convenience" was a small building out back.

Besides the inn, the resort had rustic cabins, bridal trails, campgrounds, playgrounds, tennis courts, bathing lagoons, and the "Wig-wam," a covered dance pavilion. "Still's Park" soon became one of the most popular vacation spots on Puget Sound. Visitors from Seattle and Tacoma arrived on board paddlewheel steamboats to enjoy the facilities, the great outdoors, and the social life. One of the most colorful personalities at the resort was Judge Still himself. An old black-and-white photo (now displayed in the inn's lobby) shows the judge to have been a short, pale, balding man in sideburns and spectacles, who seems a little lost in his voluminous black robes. Yet local residents described him as an outspoken, confident, almost flamboyant character, a "gay bachelor" who loved dancing and flirting with the ladies. He never married.

Though Still owned the resort, all the work of running it fell to manager George Virtue. After a few years, Virtue bought the resort from Still. It remained in the hands of the Virtue family until the Great Depression. Since then, the resort has been owned by several families. It was run by John and Rachel Colby for several years in the early 1960s, until they sold it to John's niece Shirlie Stone and her husband Steve.

Taking over the inn in 1964, the Stone family rented out the building's front rooms and lived in rooms in the back. When demand for rooms was high, the Stone's young son, John Colby Stone, and his brother had to give up their bedrooms and sleep in a tent outside. John tried to regain control of his room by hanging his model airplanes from the ceiling. He thought that if visitors realized they were taking a little boy's bedroom, they'd feel guilty and want a different room. The plan backfired, however. John's room became a favorite with many visitors, who specifically requested the room with the model airplanes.

John Stone never expected to take over the family business, but after graduating from college he came home to Whidbey Island to help his parents run the inn until they could find a qualified buyer and retire. Within a few years John himself became that buyer, purchasing the inn in 1980.

During its thirty years of ownership by the Colby/Stone family, the Captain Whidbey Inn (as it is now called) has undergone gradual improvements but few major changes. Most significant has been the development of the land surrounding the inn. Earlier owners sold off the resort's land until its 160 acres dwindled down to seven. The Stone family, however, has bought back some of the property and built cabins, condo-like "lagoon units" and vacation cottages. There's even a big wooden gazebo, modeled after the "Wig-wam" dancing pavilion built in Judge Still's time.

The Captain Whidbey Inn today

Walls of beautifully polished madrona logs give the inn a rustic warmth, as if you were a pioneer on the edge of civilization. Actually, the accommodations inside are totally civilized: high-backed armchairs, spacious rooms with electric heating, feather beds with down comforters. (If you've never slept on a feather bed, you must try it. It's a heavenly experience.)

JOHN AND ROBERTA WOLCOTT, COURTESY OF THE CAPTAIN WHIDBEY INN

To make this suite's king-size, four-poster bed, the innkeepers used weathered timbers from the railing of their outdoor deck.

Room 4, a suite, contains a magnificent four-poster king-size bed. To build it, the Stones needed wood with a smooth, weathered look, so they took apart the railing on their outside deck and used the beams to build the bed.

Rooms throughout the inn are filled with antique treasures from around the world. Along the main hallway, for example, you'll find a 200-year-old spinning wheel, an admiral's uniform, and old sailors chests. An elaborate model ship, which a local sailor carved out of a fencepost with his pocket knife, is on display in the modest dining room. Dinners here, always available for guests and sometimes for non-guests, include fresh local seafood, such as salmon croquettes or Penn Cove mussels steamed in white wine ($15-20). Hot breakfasts feature entree's like omlettes and French toast, as well as homemade granola, fresh fruit, and hot scones. Drinks are served in "the Chart Room," a bar with such a wild decor that I won't even attempt to describe it.

What to do on Whidbey Island

Only a few minutes away from the inn is historic **Coupeville**, one of the oldest towns in Washington. There you'll find quaint **shops**, nineteenth century **houses**, and several authentic **blockhouses**, built by early pioneers as protection against Indian attacks. The **Island County Historical Society Museum** displays exhibits about Puget Sound's past. Whidbey Island's spectacular scenery can perhaps best be enjoyed in **Ebey's Landing**, a rural community that has become our nation's first national historic preserve. **Fort Casey**, once a coastal defense installation, is now a state park and historical monument, with bunkers, gun emplacements, and a lighthouse.

Room Rates: Inn rooms $85-95, inn suites $145-155. Other accommodations $125-250. Breakfast included with all accomodations.

Reservations: Recommended four to six weeks in advance during the summer.

Restrictions: No pets. No children or smoking allowed in main inn. Two night minimum for all weekends.

Room Features: No television sets, telephones, or private bathrooms in main inn.

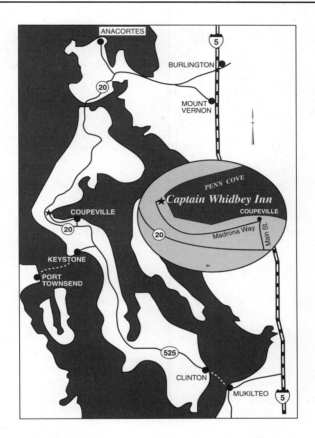

How to get there

To get to Whidbey Island, you can drive south on State Route 20 near Anacortes, or take the ferry to Keystone from Port Townsend on the Olympic Peninsula. The most common route, though, is to take the ferry from Mukilteo to Clinton. Then drive north on State Route 525, which becomes State Route 20. When you get to Coupeville, turn right onto Main Street. Follow it through town, then turn left onto Madrona Way. Take this road around Penn Cove and turn right onto Captain Whidbey Inn Road.

**George Starrett built this mansion as a gift for his new bride, Ann —
and to show off his carpentry skills to his clients.**

Starrett Mansion Inn

744 Clay Street
Port Townsend, WA 98368
(206) 385-3205

History

In 1889, George Starrett gave his wife Ann a truly impressive wedding present — two years late.

Ann Starrett was the daughter of a Port Townsend pioneer who had become one of the town's most prominent citizens, serving as postmaster, sheriff, and probate judge. Her new husband had arrived in 1885, leaving Maine to seek his fortune in the Northwest. In Port Townsend, he ran the town's sawmill and found his true calling as an architect and builder.

Starrett arrived in the middle of Port Townsend's boom years. Residents were convinced their busy seaport would soon become a major metropolis. All they needed were railroads to connect them with the rest of the country for Port Townsend to become the "Key City of the Puget Sound."

Meanwhile, Starrett was making a fortune building the majestic brick buildings and elegant Victorian homes that Port Townsend residents felt their great city deserved. He once bragged to the town newspaper that, since his arrival, he had built an average of one house per week — about 350 houses.

So it should come as no surprise that Starrett's gift to his beloved bride would be not merely a house, but a mansion in grand Victorian style, an architectural jewel whose beauty would outshine every other home in town. It took Starrett two years and $6,000 to complete this showpiece, its

25

fancy eaves and gables probably meant to show off his carpentry skills to prospective clients.

Running along the inside of the three-story octagonal tower was a mahogany spiral staircase, called free-floating because no pillars or other visible means of support held it up. According to the Smithsonian Institute, this is the last staircase of its kind left in the United States. On the ceiling of the tower, a local artist painted his rendition of the Four Seasons and the Four Virtues. (The town's Victorian ladies are said to have been shocked by the figure of "Winter," a skimpily dressed girl shivering in the snow.) The tower also served as an ingenious solar calendar. Four times a year, on the equinoxes and solstices, sunlight would pass through small windows in the tower, down to a pane of red glass, forming a beam of light that pointed to the appropriate season's panel.

Completed in 1889, the extravagant Starrett Mansion quickly became a center of Port Townsend life. In its richly furnished parlors, the couple entertained governors, sea captains, and foreign dignitaries. George came to hold many important civic offices, including seats on the school board and the city council. Ann was one of the founders of the town's first library.

Then hard times came to Port Townsend. The much-anticipated railroad never came: the Oregon Improvement Company, which had promised to connect Port Townsend with the Union Pacific Railroad, went bankrupt in 1891. Seattle, not Port Townsend, became the center of shipping and big business in the Northwest. Olympia became the seat of Washington's government. Port Townsend was all but forgotten. Today Port Townsend is one of only four remaining Victorian seaports in America that has preserved its architectural heritage, a town frozen in time.

As the town's economy crumbled, hardship also visited the Starrett family. When the building business declined, Starrett began making money in less respectable ways, like undertaking. It was rumored that he also smuggled rum, often sneaking it into the country in coffins. The family moved out of the mansion and, when Ann Starrett died in 1914, Starrett married her seamstress. He never moved back into the mansion.

All but abandoned, the mansion was converted into a boarding house. Many soldiers stayed there while stationed at nearby Fort Worden. It wasn't until the 1960s that people began to recognize the beauty of the

Starrett Mansion and the other old Victorian houses that were a legacy of Port Townsend's boom years. In 1970, the Starrett Mansion was placed on the National Register of Historic Places. It has exchanged hands eight times, each new family doing a share to restore the house to its former glory. Architectural enthusiasts now recognize the Starrett Mansion as one of the most important Victorian houses in America.

The Starrett Mansion Inn today

When current owners Bob and Edel Sokol bought the mansion in 1986, it was in good condition but empty of furnishings. To create their bed-and-breakfast inn, they filled the house with an eclectic collection of antiques, mostly from the Renaissance and Victorian periods. Five of the eleven guest rooms are decorated in authentic Victorian style. Other rooms are simpler, more contemporary, and less expensive — except for the honeymoon suite, which has its own hot soaking tub.

It is the mansion's public rooms that are the most spectacular, whirling with lush, rich colors. Fine Oriental rugs cover dark hardwood floors. Painted vases overflow with bright silk flower arrangements. Velvet love seats nestle into corners gently lit by tasseled lamps. A bouquet of peacock feathers is gathered into a blue Chinese bowl on a carved wooden mantel-piece. Lords and ladies dance on the face of an eighteenth century Brussels tapestry.

Yet in spite of the museum-like quality of the mansion, the Sokols encourage their guests to explore the house and make themselves at home in its parlors. In the morning, they serve a rich breakfast often featuring stuffed French toast.

What to do in Port Townsend

After you've checked in to the Starrett Mansion Inn, take a walk around the neighborhood to see the other **Victorian homes**, many of them offering bed and breakfast and/or tours during the day. The 1868 **Rothchild House** holds the original furnishings of the Rothchild family and serves as Washington's smallest state park. The stairs at the southeast end of Taylor Street will take you down to historic **Water Street**. There the stately brick buildings house antique stores, book shops, cafes, trendy boutiques, and quirky art galleries. At the northeast end of town, you'll find the 1891 brick city hall, now home to the **Jefferson County Historical Museum**. Driving north, visit the Coastal Artillery Museum and the Commanding Officer's House in **Fort Worden State Park**. The miles of shoreline that stretch from Port Townsend to Fort Worden also are good for **beachcombing**.

Room Rates: $70-185, breakfast included.

Restrictions: No smoking, no pets, no children under twelve.

Reservations: Advanced reservations are recommended, especially if you want to stay in a particular room.

Room Features: No television sets, no telephones, almost all rooms have private bathrooms.

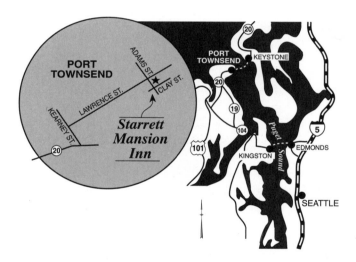

How to get there

To get to Port Townsend, you can either take the ferry from Edmunds to Kingston, then drive west on Highway 104, north on Highway 19, and north on Highway 20, or take the ferry directly to Port Townsend from Keystone on Whidbey Island. Once in town, go north on Kearney Street. Turn right on Lawrence Street and follow it up the hill. Drive for about twelve blocks and turn right onto Adams Street; the Starrett Mansion is on the corner of Adams and Clay.

Lake Crescent Lodge

National Park Concessions
HC 62, Box 11
Port Angeles, WA 98362-9798
(206) 928-3211

History

Since 1895, one of Lake Crescent's most famous residents has been a fish.

At that time, the town of Port Angeles was in trouble. Banks closed; the economy declined. A newspaperman developed a plan to save the city: He invited Rear Admiral Lester A. Beardslee, Commander of the Pacific Squadron of the U.S. Navy, to come for a visit. Much to everyone's surprise, he came — and brought five battleships with him.

The town entertained its guests with formal dinners, dances, and parades, but what most impressed the admiral was a fishing trip he took to Lake Crescent. Beardslee, a dedicated trout fisherman, could hardly believe the size of the giant trout he caught there; some weighed more than ten pounds. That subspecies of trout, believed to live only in Lake Crescent, was named in the admiral's honor, and today is called Beardslee's trout.

After his visit, Beardslee chose Port Angeles as an official training station of the U.S. Pacific Squadron — a decision that helped stimulate the town's economy. At the same time, the admiral's much-publicized praise of Lake Crescent attracted fishermen from far and wide. A 1903 magazine article reported that "The fisherman is king at Lake Crescent ... The mere guest who comes to breathe the fresh air, walk among the pines, feast lazily on the kaleidoscope scenery, or perchance peevishly await the arrival of

On the shores of remote Lake Crescent, this old-fashioned lodge has been welcoming fishermen and nature lovers for almost eighty years.

the meal hour, must expect to hear fish-talk at all hours of the day or night...."

Still, as this reporter implied, not all of Lake Crescent's visitors came for the trout. The silver lake surrounded by lush mountainsides offered a secluded getaway for weary city dwellers. Over the course of thirty years, some fifteen resort hotels were built along the lakefront, the first one constructed in 1891. While getting back to nature, guests enjoyed home-cooked meals, rowboat rides, and formal gardens.

The most posh resort on the lake was Singer's Tavern, built by Avery and Julia Singer in 1915 at a cost of $50,000. This two-story wooden lodge, covered in cedar shingles, had a wide wraparound porch from which guests could admire a panoramic view of the lake and mountains. Until a road to the lodge was completed in 1922, tourists had to ride back and forth across the lake on Mr. Singer's private launch. On the resort's carefully tended grounds, visitors played tennis, horseshoes, croquet, and golf. Dinners were black-tie affairs; even the busboys wore formal attire. After supper, visitors danced on the porch to music from a player piano.

The tavern's classy accommodations were put to the test on September 30, 1937, with the arrival of President Franklin D. Roosevelt. For several years, Congress had debated a proposal to establish a large national park on the Olympic Peninsula. Now the president came to see the area for himself. After dinner in the lodge dining room, Roosevelt discussed the idea and declared his enthusiastic support. Olympic National Park was created the following year.

The lodge, after thirty-six years under various private owners, was sold to the National Park Service in 1951. The park service has spent more than $1 million to improve and restore the resort. Today called the Lake Crescent Lodge, it is one of only two of the original resorts left on the lake.

The Lake Crescent Lodge today

Nestled among the ancient evergreens, the lodge looks like a turn-of-the-century farmhouse with triangular roofs, covered in gray shingles. At its heart is its rustic lobby. All around the big stone fireplace are hung Native American masks, baskets, and totem poles; the eyes of a giant elk in full antlers looks down on you. Off to the side, a long covered sundeck gives you a peerless view of the lake. The wraparound porch was walled in during the 1930s, and the "outside" wall is still covered in shingles.

Heading up the old wooden staircase and down a long wood-planked hallway, you'll find five guest rooms (the rest of the rooms are now used as the resort's offices). Accomodations are simple and old-fashioned: woven rugs, wooden armchairs, white tasssled bedspreads. The rooms are a bit small, but families will find more spacious quarters in the fireplace cottages. They were built at the same time as the lodge, and Cabin 34 is rumored to have been the one Roosevelt used.

In its first days, the lodge was known for its formal dinners. Today the dining room is more casual and serves mainly seafood dinners like jumbo shrimp and Dungeness crab cakes for about $11-16.

What to do around Lake Crescent

Lake Crescent is a beautiful place for **beach-combing** and **boating**; you can borrow one of the resort's rowboats or launch your own boat at a public ramp. Miles of **hiking trails** stretch through the mountains and rain forests of Olympic National Park, including the nearby **Marymere Falls Nature Trail**. For an interesting day trip, drive up to **Hurricane Ridge** to enjoy the scenery and wildlife. In **Port Angeles**, you can visit a modern fine arts center, a rare antique steam locomotive, and a historical museum in the Clallam County Courthouse. And, of course, there's always **trout fishing**.

Room Rates: Historic lodge rooms $65, fireplace cottages $117-127 (more modern cottages and motel-type lodge rooms are less expensive).

Reservations: Advance reservations are always recommended.

Restrictions: No children allowed in historic lodge rooms.

Room Features: No television sets, no telephones, no private baths in historic lodge.

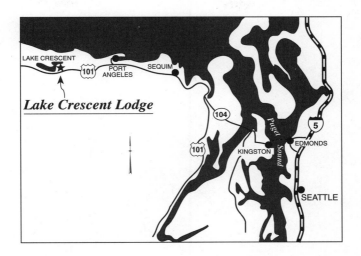

How to get there

From Interstate 5, take the ferry across Puget Sound from Edmonds to Kingston. Take 104 west until it connects with State 101. Follow 101 north, then west, passing Sequim and Port Angeles. Lake Crescent and the lodge are about a half-hour's drive further on 101.

Lumber, bricks, and glass had to be hauled fifty miles over dirt roads to become the classic Lake Quinault Lodge.

Lake Quinault Lodge

P.O. Box 7
Quinault, WA 98575
(206) 288-2571

History

According to local legend, the Lake Quinault Lodge was built on a bet.

Other, earlier lodges had been built in the heart of the Olympic Peninsula, as settlers were drawn to this secluded wilderness with its ice-capped mountains, ocean beaches, and lush rainforests. In 1890, the Olson brothers, sons of a pioneer family, built a log hotel near the banks of Lake Quinault. For decades, it sheltered first migrating travelers, then outdoor-loving tourists. The hotel was so successful that the Olson brothers built three other hotels in the Olympic Mountains.

By 1923, so many tourists were driving to Lake Quinault that more rooms were needed. An annex was built, complete with its own kitchen, dining hall, coffee shop, and sleeping quarters. It still houses visitors today.

Later that year, the main log hotel accidentally caught fire and burned to the ground. It was obvious that the small annex wouldn't be able to hold all of Lake Quinault's guests — especially to Frank McNeil, a linotype operator for the *Seattle Post-Intelligencer*. Recognizing a golden opportunity, McNeil obtained permission from the Forest Service to construct a new hotel on the site. McNeil didn't have the money to build the magnificent mountain lodge he had in mind, so he began to tour the Aberdeen/Hoquiam area, hoping to find someone to invest in his plan.

He found Ralph Emerson, a wealthy lumberman. As the story goes,

Emerson made the legendary bet, wagering against a rival lumber baron that he could complete the lodge in record time. That would explain the builders' frantic pace. Construction went on twenty-four hours a day, employing dozens of craftsmen from all over the Northwest. Lumber, bricks, glass, plumbing, fixtures, and furniture all had to be hauled fifty miles over dirt roads to reach Lake Quinault. To ornament the informal lobby, workmen built a wide brick fireplace and hand-stenciled the ceiling beams with colorful designs of ducks, horses, wolves, and Indian hunters. The long, curving lodge, covered in rough cedar shingles, cost the extraordinary amount of $90,000. We can only hope that it was worth it to Emerson, and that he won the bet. From start to finish, the Lake Quinault Lodge was completed in just ten weeks.

Although the lodge was completed in 1926, the perfect opportunity to show it off didn't arrive until more than ten years later. On October 1, 1937, the day after his visit to Lake Crescent, President Franklin D. Roosevelt came to the Lake Quinault Lodge. He was touring the area to evaluate the idea of establishing a national park on the Olympic Peninsula. At Lake Quinault, the president enjoyed a lunch of broiled salmon with egg sauce, ripe olives, pickled peaches, clam chowder, whipped potatoes, green peas, cottage cheese, currant jelly, hot rolls, and buttermilk. For decades, the proprietors of the Lake Quinault Lodge have boasted that it was the lodge and the lunch that persuaded FDR to create Olympic National Park in 1938.

In sixty-five years, the Lake Quinault Lodge has grown and evolved to keep pace with the times. In the 1970s, a new wing of the lodge was added, along with a swimming pool, a recreation room, and a row of sixteen modern "fireplace units." A local woman carved, with a power saw, the totem pole-like rain gauge, whose bone marker shows how much rain has fallen on Quinault throughout the year. After being run by private owners for decades, the lodge was purchased by a national company called ARA Leisure Services in January of 1988. Yet in many ways Lake Quinault remains unchanged: a secluded, classic lodge where travelers come to enjoy the quiet beauty of the Olympic Peninsula.

The Lake Quinault Lodge today

Rooms at the lodge are large and comfortable, though a bit plain. The wood furnishings are reproduction pieces that suit the mood well. Ruffled comforters and warm carpets make your lodgings cozy, while ceiling fans and cast-iron radiators help maintain the old-fashioned atmosphere. A few modern touches include private bathrooms, contemporary art prints, and electric clocks beside the beds. More rustic lodgings can be found in the eight rooms of the annex. Their walls paneled in plain wood, these rooms are decorated with antique iron beds and matching furnishings.

Heading back to the main lodge, you cross a sweeping green lawn and pass through a back door into the lobby. It feels like a family's living room, with its great wicker chairs parked in front of the brick fireplace. The gift shop, however, overflows into the room, making it feel a bit cluttered. Slightly fancier is the dining room, decorated with antique glass chandeliers, lacy white curtains, and watercolors with a Native American theme. Guests will be more impressed by the splendid view of Lake Quinault, and by the menu. The dining room specializes in seafood dinners, including stuffed mountain trout, jumbo prawns, and Quinault River salmon, served fresh for $15-20. Take an extra look at the alcove in the corner, where Roosevelt ate his much-celebrated salmon lunch.

What to do around Lake Quinault

Inside the lodge, you may want to spend time enjoying the **heated pool** and **sauna** downstairs. Then head out to explore the **rain forests**. There are many popular **hiking trails** through the forest, including the five-mile **Lake Quinault trail**. No water-skiing is allowed on the lake, but quieter **boating** is fine. **Fishing** is permitted with a license from the Quinault Indians. During the summer, pontoon boats take guests on **tours of the lake**. Many public **ocean beaches** dot the shores to the northwest. In Neah Bay, visit the **Makah Cultural and Research Center**, containing a vast collection of Northwest Native American artifacts. Also north is the **Hoh Rain Forest**, considered one of the most beautiful places on the peninsula, which has its own **visitors center**. The nearest cities are **Hoquiam** and **Aberdeen**, about forty miles to the south.

Room Rates: Main lodge $75-105, suites $120-170. Lakeside Inn $85-115, suites $170-210. Annex $60-85.

Reservations: Recommended two to three months in advance for summer.

Restrictions: Both smoking and non-smoking rooms are available. Children are welcome.

Room Features: Private bathrooms and clock radios. No television sets or telephones.

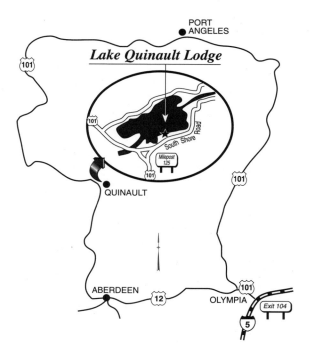

How to get there

To get to Lake Quinault, take Highway 101 either south from Port Angeles or north from Aberdeen (Highway 101 connects with Interstate 5 near Olympia). At Milepost 125, go northeast on South Shore Road and drive for two miles. The lodge will be on your left.

Four Seasons Olympic Hotel

411 University Street
Seattle, WA 98101
(206) 621-1700

History

Perhaps more than any other hotel in the country, the Olympic was a community effort.

In 1920, Seattle was in a depression. Throughout World War I, government orders for warships and other vessels had kept Seattle's shipyards busy. At the end of the war, however, those orders stopped abruptly. Seattle needed a new source of income. At that time, many large companies and organizations were holding big, expensive annual conventions. Seattle wanted to attract some of that business, but it didn't have a hotel big enough or grand enough to compete with other cities. So, with thousands of people out of work, the Seattle business community decided to build a huge luxury hotel.

The first problem was where to build it. Many people argued that in should be in the retail district, on First and Second avenues, or on the Denny Regrade, to the north. They finally settled on a piece of land, owned by the University of Washington, between Fourth and Fifth avenues. The university's original campus had been located there until it was moved to its current home on Lake Washington.

The next problem was money. To pay for the multi-million-dollar hotel, 400 volunteer salespeople sold bonds to the public. Teams competed to sell the most; a scoreboard nine feet high and forty-two feet long displayed each day's sales. Seattleites responded with enthusiasm, buying

Thousands of Seattle residents invested their money in building this multi-million-dollar downtown hotel.

$1.6 million in bonds during the campaign's first twenty-four hours. Eventually the fund-raising effort would bring in $5.5 million.

Every penny would be needed. The new Olympic Hotel was twelve stories high, had 617 guest rooms, and occupied almost an entire city block. Its fashionable Italian Renaissance facade was covered in bricks (almost 2,500,000 of them) and trimmed in white terra cotta. Tall, arched Palladian windows brought sunlight into the elaborate Georgian Room and the Spanish Ballroom. Golden-brown American oak, carved into pillars and balconies, fruit and flowers, paneled the classically styled lobby. Italian workmen were brought to Seattle to lay down the patterned terrazzo floors. Rooms throughout the Olympic were decorated with antique mirrors, bronze statues, and Italian and Spanish oil jars. With construction going on six days a week, ten hours a day, the hotel was completed in nine months — one month ahead of schedule.

The opening night gala, held on December 6, 1924, was a splendid affair attended by some 2,500 guests. "Seattle has never seen so many charmingly gowned women at one affair nor so many gallant escorts to admire and attend them," reported the *Seattle Times*. " . . . the vivid coloring of stunning dinner gowns, fans, and shawls and the sparkle of jewels made a gorgeous picture and the music of four orchestras scattered through the hotel contributed to the thrill of the spectacle."

From that night on, the Olympic was the gathering place of choice for Seattle's social elite. Every Monday, the city's most fashionable ladies met for luncheon in the Georgian Room; local newspapers would report the next day who was seen with whom and what they were wearing. Seattle radio stations broadcast music from the Olympic's orchestras all over the Northwest. Some of the hotel's most prominent guests included six U.S. presidents, Ethiopia's Emperor Haile Selassie, Japan's Crown Prince Akihito, and the Duke of Edinburgh, Prince Philip of England.

By the late 1970s, the Olympic needed a restoration. The University of Washington, which still owned the property, had to decide what to do. Strong public support of the hotel, a Washington state legislature resolution in its favor, and the Olympic's placement on the National Register of Historic Places, all helped to convince the university that the hotel was worth preserving. The Olympic was leased to Four Seasons Hotels, which began an extensive two-year renovation. Besides restoring details such as the hotel's fine woodwork and crystal chandeliers, major changes included the construction of larger guest rooms, a new circular drive and grand entrance, a new restaurant, and a modern exercise room, the Solarium. The restoration cost a total of $60 million — more than ten times the cost of constructing the original Olympic Hotel.

The Olympic Hotel today

Rooms at the Olympic are posh, decorated in light, romantic shades of blue, creme, or rose. Contemporary in style, they're furnished with brass lamps, thick carpets, and furniture in teak and mahogany. In the hotel's suites, sitting rooms with embroidered armchairs are separated from the bedrooms by curtained French doors. Because of the Olympic's downtown location, there's some street noise, but most of the rooms have nice views of the city.

The finery here is subdued rather than showy. Take the lobby, for example. The woodwork doesn't need to be trimmed in gold; it is lovely in itself, the leafy swirls and scrollwork complementing the slender Corinthian columns. More flamboyant is the Georgian Room, decked in crystal and long tablecloths, where banquet-like meals of veal and venison are served with style ($20-30). For less formal affairs, try the Garden Court, a greenhouse-like restaurant that serves soup and sandwiches, or Shuckers oyster bar.

What to do in downtown Seattle

Within walking distance of the Olympic Hotel are the **Seattle Art Museum,** to the south, and Seattle's **shopping district,** centered around **Westlake Center,** to the north. Much of the city's entertainment takes place at **Seattle Center,** built for the 1962 World's Fair with an amusement park and the Space Needle. The **Seattle Opera, Seattle Symphony, Pacific Northwest Ballet,** and several theater companies all perform here. You'll also want to visit Seattle's **waterfront** and the historic **Pike Place Market.** About seven blocks south of the hotel is **Pioneer Square,** Seattle's turn-of-the-century commercial district, its Romanesque brick buildings now housing shops, art galleries, and night clubs.

Room Rates: $135-300.

Reservations: Should be made as early as possible.

Restrictions: Both children and pets are allowed. Smoking and non-smoking floors are available.

Room Features: Private bathrooms, television sets, clock radios, two telephones per room.

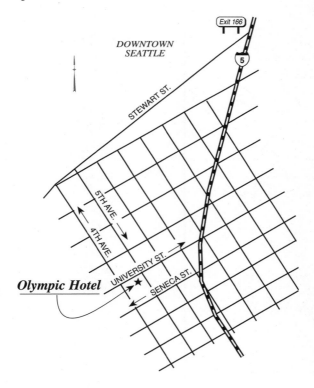

How to get there
From Interstate 5, take Exit 166 onto Stewart Street. Turn left onto Fifth Avenue and continue for five blocks. Take a right onto Seneca Street, then another right onto Fourth Avenue. Turn right again onto University. The hotel's driveway will be on your right.

43

Master architect Harlan Thomas designed this Italian Renaissance hotel in imitation of one of his favorite buildings in Italy.

Sorrento Hotel

900 Madison Street
Seattle, WA 98104
(206) 622-6400

History

It began with a vacation.

The vacation was a trip to Italy, and the man enjoying it was Harlan Thomas, one of the Northwest's most respected turn-of-the-century architects. He visited Sorrento, a city overlooking the Bay of Naples, and stayed in the Sorrento Hotel, a renovated castle hundreds of years old. Thomas fell in love with the building, sketched it, and brought his memories of it home to Seattle.

There, Thomas was building apartments on Queen Anne Hill when he was approached by Samuel Rosenburg, a successful clothing merchant who had decided to go into the hotel business. He had bought property on First Hill, overlooking downtown and Puget Sound, and commissioned Thomas to design the hotel. Thomas, admiring the view of Elliott Bay, was reminded of the Bay of Naples. He designed the hotel in the style of the Italian Renaissance, and named it "The Sorrento" after his favorite hotel in Italy.

Construction began in 1908. The hotel was built in the shape of a "V," centered around a grand entrance and an Italian garden. The brick exterior of the seven-story hotel was ornamented in white stone, with four square towers along the top. Thomas paneled the Sorrento's lobby in fine Honduran mahogany, and crowned the room with a hand-crafted tile fireplace. Thomas would go on to design the corner building of the Pike Place

Market and to become the first dean of architecture at the University of Washington, but perhaps Thomas' greatest legacy was the Sorrento.

The hotel opened in early spring of 1909, in time for the Alaska-Yukon-Pacific Exposition that summer. Even after the fair had come and gone, the Sorrento was a success, attracting such famous families as the Vanderbilts and the Guggenheims. A 1919 brochure described the Sorrento as "Seattle's Exclusive Hostelry."

Like many fine hotels, the Sorrento began to decline during the Great Depression. Rosenburg had hoped his two sons would take over the hotel someday, but they were interested in agriculture, not hotels. So Rosenburg traded the Sorrento for the Bear Creek pear orchards near Medford, Oregon. Ever heard of "Harry & David"? That's right — those pear orchards would one day become the multi-million dollar gift-fruit business that today bears the names of Rosenburg's two sons. Rosenburg was widely quoted as saying "I traded a lemon for a pear."

Perhaps Rosenburg was right — at the time. Throughout the 1940s and 1950s, the Sorrento was mainly known not as a hotel, but as a restaurant. Stylish couples came to the "Top of the Town" on the top floor for "prime rib with a view." The hotel itself, however, was becoming run-down and was operated as much as an apartment building as an hotel. When the "Top of the Town" closed in the 1970s, the Sorrento's future looked bleak.

Two Seattle businessmen who bought the Sorrento were faced with a choice: tear down the old hotel or renovate it completely. Fortunately, they chose the latter, joining forces to give the Sorrento a $4.5 million facelift. Besides adding new plumbing and electrical systems, they redesigned the Sorrento's interior, reducing the number of rooms from 150 to 76. The hotel's exterior was cleaned and repaired, the front garden replaced by a circular driveway that would allow guests to drive up to the canopied entrance. The crowning touch — an antique Italian fountain — was found, after a long search, not in Italy, but in Canada.

Since the Sorrento's reopening in 1981, it has reclaimed its role of "Seattle's Exclusive Hostelry." Known as a small hotel that provides both privacy and exceptional service, the Sorrento has become a favorite stopping place for traveling celebrities. Its list of past VIP guests includes Matt Dillon, Jay Leno, Lily Tomlin, Gregory Hines, Beau Bridges, Loretta Swit, and Raymond Burr, as well as many prominent figures in the music world, such as Harry Belafonte, Reba McIntyre, Debbie Gibson, Ozzie Ozborn, David Bowie, Kenny Rogers, Madonna, and the band Nirvana. Several movies have been filmed here, including scenes for the 1993 summer hit *Sleepless In Seattle*. Even some of the hotel's old-time famous guests might be found at the Sorrento: it's said that the ghost of Cornelius Vanderbilt still haunts room 408, where guests have heard him moving objects around.

COURTESY OF THE SORRENTO HOTEL

Brick walls, fine china, and soft lighting give the Hunt Club an intimate, romantic atmosphere.

The Sorrento Hotel today

Today's Sorrento prides itself on its impeccable service. In the evening, the staff turn down your bed, put some soft music on the stereo, and lay out a white terry cloth robe for you. On cold winter nights, guests find hot water bottles placed under their covers to warm their feet. Such small touches of luxury have qualified the Sorrento as a Preferred Hotel — a title given to only 108 hotels around the world.

For the ultimate night in the Sorrento, you'd have to stay in the Penthouse Suite. There's a large bedroom, two bathrooms, a kitchenette, a library, a living room with a marble firplace and a baby grand piano, and a private outdoor deck with a hot tub. The cost? One thousand dollars a night.

If that's beyond your budget, you can experience the Sorrento's charm in one of the smaller rooms or suites. They're warm and spacious, graciously decorated with a mixture of contemporary and antique-style furniture. Asian paintings add an Oriental motif to the European furnishings.

No discussion of the Sorrento would be complete without some mention of the Hunt Club. The brick-lined walls of the first-floor restaurant help create a cozy, candlelite atmosphere. Meals there aren't cheap (entrees cost $20-25) but they are delicious and gorgeously prepared, tender meat dishes in light sauces. In the Fireside Room, seated in an embroidered armchair, you can take tea in the afternoon or dessert from 3 p.m. until midnight.

What to do around Seattle

The Sorrento sits high on First Hill, where many of the city's wealthiest residents built their homes at the turn of the century. Most notable is the **Stimson-Green Mansion**, now open for tours. Also nearby are the 1907 Baroque **Saint James Cathedral** and the1891 **Trinity Episcopal Church**. Other mansions were built on Capitol Hill, home of beautiful **Volunteer Park** and the **Seattle Art Museum**.

Architecture fans will want to visit the eclectic campus of the **University of Washington**, while history buffs should see the **Museum of History and Industry** in Montlake. On the other side of town, to the south, you'll find the **International District**, the historic center of Seattle's Asian-American community. Further north, there's the **Chittenden Locks** on the **Lake Washington Ship Canal**.

Room Rates: Rooms $130-160, suites $170-350.

Restrictions: Smoking allowed on two floors only.

Reservations: Always recommended at least one month in advance, especially for weekends and during the summer.

Room Features: Private bathrooms, stereos, television sets, telephones.

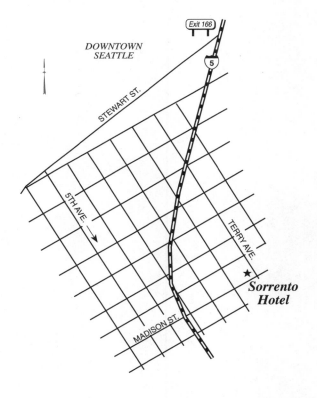

How to get there
From Interstate 5, take Exit 166 onto Stewart Street. Turn left onto Fifth Avenue and head south until you reach Madison Street. Then take a left and cross over the freeway. The hotel will be on your left, at the corner of Terry Avenue and Madison Street.

CHRISTINE UMMEL

**The Moore House, now a pleasant bed-and-breakfast inn, originally
housed turn-of-the-century railroad workers.**

Moore House

P.O. Box 629
South Cle Elum, WA 98943
(509) 674-5939

History

Jim Benson worked as a brakeman for the Chicago, Milwaukee, St. Paul, and Pacific Railroad (called the "Milwaukee Road" for short). Fellow crewmen nicknamed him "Tycoon" for his habit of following the stock market, but Benson was a hard worker. He often worked sixteen hours at a stretch to earn his full day's wages — $7.37 in 1946. One winter's night, Benson's train was thundering down Snoqualmie Pass when it hit a snow-slide blocking the tracks. The first car flipped over, sending the train tobogganing down the mountainside. Benson walked away from the accident, dazed but unharmed, and was soon back to work on another train.

As the Milwaukee Road wound its way through the Northwest, its terminals were built 100 miles apart. For conductors, brakemen, firemen, and engineers, a day's work meant covering those 100 miles from one terminal to the next. Most railroad workers in this area lived in Tacoma, to the west, or Othello, to the east. When they stopped for the night in Cle Elum, in the middle, they needed somewhere to sleep.

In most places, the railroad company contracted with a hotel to house the workers. In the little mining town of South Cle Elum, high in the Cascade mountains, however, no such hotel existed. So in 1909 the Milwaukee Road built its own housing, just west of the railroad depot. The bunkhouse was nothing fancy: It was built by bridge carpenters out of the same rough timbers they used to build railroad trestles. The whole building cost only $1,420.

51

Eight years after its construction, the bunkhouse had to be moved to make room for equipment that would electrify the Milwaukee Road lines. Temporary railroad tracks were laid down across a field. Then the bunkhouse was lifted onto a flatcar and rolled to its present location. Even though the trains had electricity by 1917, the bunkhouse didn't get electricity until ten years later. When an addition was built in 1920, the bunkhouse had twenty-eight bedrooms, but only two bathrooms.

In spite of the primitive accommodations, crewmen had to pay to spend the night in the bunkhouse (it usually cost them only a quarter). Besides sleeping, they spent time in the noisy, smoky lobby, talking and playing cards. During the 1950s, the lobby also featured a television set with a coin-operated timer. The men had to keep plunking coins into the slot or it would shut off midway through their favorite TV shows. Throughout the building's history, there was always a bunkhouse custodian around to enforce the railroad's rule of conduct: no drinking, no gambling, and no women. Naturally, all three rules were broken from time to time.

The bunkhouse's decades of faithful service came to an end in 1974. Faster, modern trains enabled crewmen to work from Tacoma to Othello, and vice versa, in one twelve-hour stretch. The South Cle Elum terminal was closed, and its bunkhouse abandoned. The Milwaukee Road itself went bankrupt in 1980.

After being used as a private home for several years, the bunkhouse was sold in 1982 to Monty and Connie Moore, a Seattle couple interested in opening it as a bed-and-breakfast. By then in a state of complete disrepair, the building took five years to rehabilitate. Retired Milwaukee Road workers, happy to see the old bunkhouse brought back to life, gave the Moores the souvenirs they had kept from a lifetime working aboard trains. Though now owned by a different family, the Moore House is still decorated with this vast collection of railroad memorabilia. Today each guest room bears the name of a railroad worker, like Jim Benson, who stayed in the Milwaukee Road bunkhouse.

The Moore House today

Milwaukee Road crewmen who visited their old bunkhouse now might find it a bit feminine for their taste. (Walls in the original bunkhouse were painted an ugly dark green.) Today the guest rooms are decorated in light

colors with ruffled curtains, old-fashioned wallpaper, and homey oak furniture. Trains are everywhere — train posters, model trains, train puzzles,
train lanterns, vintage photographs of trains. A mannequin in full conduc-
tor regalia greets guests as they walk down the hallway.

The railroad motif continues down the stairs into the informal sitting
room, where couches and rocking chairs circle an old-fashioned wood-
burning stove. In the plain, wood-paneled dining room next door, simple
but delicious breakfasts are served, such as spiced waffles and fresh melon,
or scrambled eggs and sausage. An outdoor hot tub is available for guests'
use year-round.

Also outdoors are some of the most unusual accommodations at the
Moore House: two remodeled train cabooses. These brightly colored railroad
cars have been furnished with families in mind; they can sleep as many as
five people and have their own television sets, refrigerators, and sundecks.

What to do around Cle Elum

By taking a short walk through the field behind the Moore House, you
can explore the ruins of the **Milwaukee Road depot and substation**. The
small town of Cle Elum has several shops and restaurants, as well as a
unique **Historical Telephone Museum**. Most visitors come to the Cascade
Mountains to enjoy outdoor activities, like **hiking**, **skiing**, **mountain biking**, and **river-rafting**, making nearby **Iron Horse State Park** and **Lake
Easton State Park** especially popular. The hamlet of **Roslyn**, well-known
as the setting for TV's "Northern Exposure," was a coal-mining town, its
twenty-five historic **cemeteries** giving testimony to the variety of immigrants that came to the Northwest looking for work. **Liberty**, also nearby,
was a gold-mining town. The closest city is **Ellensburg**.

Room Rates: Rooms $33-71, honeymoon suite $105, cabooses $95-105.

Reservations: Recommended a few weeks in advance for weekends.

Restrictions: Children welcome. Smoking allowed in lobby only.

Room Features: No telephones, no television sets. Some private bathrooms.

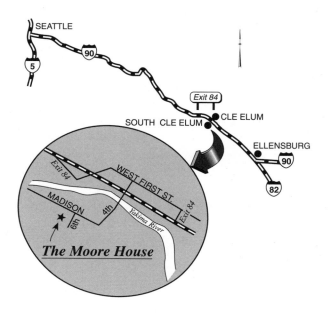

How to get there

From Interstate 90, take Exit 84 for Cle Elum. Stay on the town's main street, West First Street, then turn left onto Fourth Avenue. After you cross the Yakima River and enter South Cle Elum, make a right turn onto Madison, then a left onto Sixth Avenue. The Moore House will be a large blue building to your right.

Davenport Hotel

807 W Sprague Avenue
Spokane, WA 99201
(509) 455-8888

History

Journalist Will Irwin reportedly once said, "There are only two outstanding deluxe hotels in the world, the Davenport in Spokane and Shepeards in Cairo."

For three decades, the Davenport Hotel defined luxury in the American West. It opened its doors to Queen Marie of Romania, Prince Olaf of Norway, General Pershing, General Marshall, Charles Lindbergh, Mahatma Gandhi, and every U.S. president from Taft to Kennedy. Will Rogers called it "the best spot to stay outside of my Oklahoma." Yet the man behind this opulent hotel reportedly arrived in Spokane in 1889 with only $1.25 in his pocket.

Few rags-to-riches tales are as dramatic as the story of Louis Davenport. At age twenty-one, he left his middle-class family in Kansas and headed west, ending up some 1,500 miles away in Spokane, Washington. A terrible fire that year had destroyed much of the city, and Davenport earned enough money helping with the cleanup to buy a small plot of land. He pitched a tent and opened "Davenport's Famous Waffle Foundry," a restaurant specializing in — what else? — waffles.

In one year, Davenport earned enough to start a real restaurant. Decorated with fluted Corinthian columns, the restaurant came to be called the "Italian Gardens" because it overflowed with flower arrangements. Over the next twenty years, Davenport worked tirelessly at cultivating his restaurant: adding more space; upgrading the decor; covering the outside in a

CHRISTINE UMMEL

Under his careful supervision, Louis Davenport's restaurant (front) and luxury hotel (back) became famous throughout America.

fanciful Spanish Mission facade — even building the "Hall of Doges," an Italian Gothic ballroom with pillars and arches resembling a medieval cathedral.

All this wasn't enough for the insatiable Louis Davenport. He dreamed of building a luxury hotel next to his famous restaurant, and sixty of the city's wealthiest businessmen had enough faith in Davenport to invest in his dream, which eventually would cost more than $2 million. Twelve stories high, the hotel would take up an entire city block. To design it, Davenport called on Kirtland Cutter, one of the most famous architects in the Northwest, whose imaginative use of classic European designs had been the basis for many of Spokane's mansions and important buildings.

For the exterior of Davenport's hotel, Cutter used a classic design: At the bottom would be a three-story base built of white sandstone, then a U-shaped shaft of red brick, crowned with a fancy capital of terra cotta arches. Inside the hotel, Cutter revealed his true genius. He modeled the huge, two-story lobby after the outdoor patio of a traditional Spanish house. Skylights of Tiffany glass, laid across massive wooden beams, were meant to recreate the sunlight through a vine-covered grape arbor. Around the lobby were not only the restaurant and the Hall of Doges, but three new ballrooms — the "Marie Antoinette Room," decorated like a wedding cake in ivory and rose; the Spanish-style "Isabella Room," its white columns trimmed in gold; and the "Elizabethan Room," paneled in oak and hung with chandeliers of sterling silver.

When every detail was complete, Davenport gave a party. Beginning on September 17, 1914, the hotel's grand opening was celebrated with three days of parades, balls, and banquets. Over the next forty years, the Davenport would serve as the center of Spokane's social and business life. It attracted large conventions to the city, and hosted countless dances, banquets, and celebrations. Friends traditionally agreed to meet by the fireplace in the Davenport's lobby, where the fire never went out. Even more famous were the hotel's silver dollars, which were polished to a bright shine before given as change to the guests. All over America, people who pulled these gleaming coins from their pockets were recognized as recent visitors of the Davenport.

The hotel played a central role in community life even in the grim days of World War II. After Japan's attack on Pearl Harbor, the lobby's skylights were painted black, as part of the city's blackout precautions. Often soldiers with no place to stay were allowed to sleep in the lobby for free. Servicemen were attracted to the Davenport's all-night coffee shop, where a plate of spaghetti, big enough for two, in a sterling silver dish cost only fifty cents.

In 1945, at age seventy-seven, Davenport sold the hotel and retired. Each successive owner promised to run the hotel according to Davenport's standards, but most of their "improvements" changed the hotel for the worse. In the 1950s, the Italian Gardens were turned into a modern cocktail lounge; a swimming pool was installed; the arches in the Hall of Doges were filled in, making the room smaller. The Davenport gradually lost its classic charm and fell into decline. Many of its owners went into debt; one was sent to prison for investment fraud.

Even though Louis Davenport died in 1951, some of the staff believe he's still watching over the hotel. All the security guards tell the same story: Late at night when the building is deserted, they hear the elevator coming up from the basement. It goes all the way to the top floor, then comes down a few floors and stops, then comes farther down and stops again. Eventually, it makes its way down to the lobby, but when the doors open, the elevator's empty. The security guards aren't frightened by the idea of a spirit in the hotel. They say it's just Louis Davenport, wandering through his hotel to make sure everything's in order.

By the 1980s, the Davenport was in serious danger. Its owners steadily lost money and wanted to sell. Several companies came forward with plans to turn the "Grand Old Lady" into a modern convention center, but all these proposals were rejected because they would sacrifice the hotel's architectural integrity. In1989, the owners went bankrupt. In spite of the efforts of the "Friends of the Davenport," it appeared the hotel was doomed.

When all looked bleakest, the Davenport Hotel found a buyer. A Hong Kong company, Sun International Hotels Ltd., bought the hotel for $5 million. While visiting Spokane, company president Patrick Ng had fallen in love with the old building, deciding to restore its classic appearance and make the Davenport a luxury hotel once more.

The Davenport Hotel today

As this guide went to press, the Davenport was closed, undergoing a $20 million restoration of its rooms, coffee shop, restaurants, four ballrooms, and lobby. The skylights above the lobby, for example, are being cleaned so the sun will shine down through them again. Patrick Ng plans to make the hotel into an international attraction, with ten floors of hotel rooms and two floors of luxury apartments. The Davenport Hotel is scheduled to reopen in the spring of 1995.

What to do in Spokane

Spokane is the second largest city in Washington, with all the usual metropolitan attractions: shopping, theaters, sporting events. The city's centerpiece is **Riverfront Park**, built for the 1974 World's Fair, where you'll find an amusement park, an ice rink, an Imax theater, a 1902 clock tower, and a 1909 carousel with hand-carved horses. To learn more about this area's past, visit the **Cheney Cowles Museum** or Gonzaga University's **Museum of Native American Cultures**. Architecture fans will want to explore the **Browne's Addition Historic District** and **The Hill**, where Spokane's wealthy built their mansions, many of them designed by Kirtland Cutter. Just outside the city, **Riverside State Park** features many hiking trails and picnic facilities.

The Davenport Hotel will be closed for renovation until the spring of 1995.

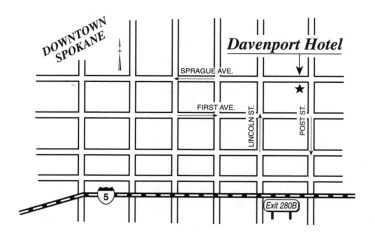

How to get there

Take Interstate 90 to Spokane and use Exit 280B to go north on Lincoln Street. The Davenport Hotel is three blocks away from the freeway, located on the city block between Lincoln Street and Post Street, First Avenue and Sprague Avenue.

Washington Hotel

Box 2
Metaline Falls, WA 99153
(509) 446-4415

History

Many small towns in the West were built around one industry, one company, or one influential family. But few towns revolved around a single man the way that Metaline Falls revolved around Lewis P. Larsen.

A young metallurgist from Denmark, Larsen came to northeast Washington in 1904. Impressed by this valley along the Pend Oreille River, with its rich deposits of lime, lead, and zinc, sprinkled with gold and silver, Larsen decided to start a town here. Over the next six years, he started the Pend Oreille Mines and Metals Company; he persuaded the Idaho and Washington Northern Railroad to build a terminal here; he helped build a dam to generate power for the town and its industries; and he persuaded the Inland Portland Cement Co. to build a cement plant here, creating dozens of steady jobs. Larsen also founded the Larsen Realty Company, which sold plots of land in the new town of Metaline Falls ("metal" for the area's metal deposits, and "falls" for a nearby waterfall).

At the center of Larsen's plan (and his town) was a hotel. Naming it for George Washington, Larsen built the three-story hotel out of local bricks and stucco at a cost of $15,000. Wanting to create an image of prosperity for the town, Larsen equipped the Washington Hotel with modern luxuries such as electricity and steam-heating.

Completed in 1910, it was a working man's hotel, home to miners, lumbermen, and cement workers. One of the managers was chef Harry

Town founder Lewis P. Larsen built the Washington Hotel as housing for local miners and cement factory workers.

Peters. To feed the hungry workers, he bought beef by the half-cow and carved it up on a chopping block in the basement. Every evening, Peters filled the long dining room table with platters of roast beer, ham, roast pork, venison, mashed potatoes, and vegetables. The huge meals were served by local high school girls, whose parents considered the Washington Hotel one of the few respectable places in town for their daughters to work.

The hotel soon became the town's social center, where many young people met their future husbands and wives. Birthday parties, weddings, christenings, and dances all took place in the main hall. During World War II, women gathered there to make bandages for the Red Cross and Christmas presents for the young men overseas.

For many years, both the town and its founder prospered. Larsen could afford to hire famous Spokane architect Kirtland Cutter to design his private home by the river. Then the town began to experience union unrest. Strikes closed many of the mines. Larsen's fortune disappeared. He lost his house and had to sell the Washington Hotel to the cement company. Although he no longer owned it, Larsen lived in a room in the hotel — until the cement company evicted him. Angry and humiliated, Larsen left town, made another fortune, and returned to build another hotel down the street, presumably motivated by vengeful dreams of putting the Washington Hotel out of business.

Years after Larsen's death in 1955, the luck of the town changed again. A flood of engineers and construction workers arrived in the 1960s to build the Boundary Dam, ten miles to the north. Workers rented basements, garages, any room they could find. The Washington Hotel's new owners, Wilson and Myrtle Lowe, were able to keep it packed to capacity. They even split up the dining room to make more bedrooms.

When the dam was completed in 1964, everyone left. The Washington Hotel, empty, was boarded up. It remained closed for seven years, until Lee McGowen came back to town. McGowen's mother had grown up in Metaline Falls and had worked as a pastry chef at the Washington Hotel, with Harry Peters teaching her how to bake pies and cakes. Although Lee McGowen was raised in Spokane, her family spent every summer relaxing in remote Metaline Falls. McGowen always loved the Washington Hotel. At age eight or nine, she bragged to a cousin that she would own the building one day. Now grown up and a successful landscape artist, McGowen's wish came true when she bought the hotel for $7,000 in 1972.

Over the next twenty years, McGowen single-handedly restored the hotel. It was a big job. Ceilings had caved in; floors were warped and bumpy. That first winter, McGowen said, she remembers sitting on the floor in front of her wood stove, crying, while the rain, dripping through three floors, fell in buckets all around her. Working room by room, sometimes wall by wall, without benefit of a single government grant or bank loan, McGowen recreated the turn-of-the-century working-class hotel, making it a haven for history buffs and artists.

Metaline Falls also has been cleaned up in recent years. The cement plant, closed in 1990, no longer showers the town with cement dust. Cleaner and prettier, Metaline Falls is now attracting tourists. If you want to know how the town's doing, just ask Lee McGowen. She's the mayor.

The Washington Hotel today

McGowen's hands-off decorating style has its pros and cons. Most elements of the hotels — the wood plank floors, for example, and the hand-stitched quilts on the old steel beds — are truly endearing. Others are simply eyesores, like the primitive bulb-on-a-string lighting in some rooms. Overall, the rooms are rustic and attractive. The nicest in the house is Room 2, often joined with Room 3 to form a suite. Larger than the other rooms, it's pleasantly decorated with dried flowers and a brass chandelier.

The hotel's facilities are also bare bones. There's no in-house restaurant, but the bakery downstairs has built a reputation on its breakfasts. A coffee maker and microwave oven are stationed in the hallway for guests' use. For entertainment, there's a homey TV room down the hall. You'll also want to explore McGowen's art gallery on the first floor, or maybe sign up for one of her art classes.

What to do in Metaline Falls

This is a small town, but it has a cafe, a movie theater, and a few shops. Plays are performed in the **Cutter Theater**, designed by Kirtland Cutter as a high school in 1912. You can also visit **Larsen's house** at the end of Fifth Street. To appreciate the area's magnificent scenery and wildlife, hike through one of the many **parks** nearby. There are summer tours and a visitors center at the **Boundary Dam. Watersports** and **boat rides** are popular along the Pend Oreille River. The area is also well-known for **fishing** and **hunting**.

Room Rates: $25 per bed per night.

Reservations: Not always necessary, but it's often a good idea to call one or two weeks in advance.

Restrictions: Small children are strongly discouraged, as is smoking.

Room Features: No television sets, no telephones, no private bathrooms.

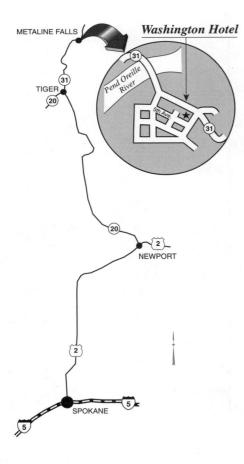

How to get there

Take Interstate 90 to Spokane, then switch onto Highway 2 headed north. When you reach Newport, take Highway 20 north for about 50 miles to Tiger. From there you take Highway 31 to Metaline Falls. At the east end of Fifth Avenue, the town's main street, you'll see the hotel on your left side.

COURTESY OF MT. RAINIER GUEST SERVICES, INC.

Newly renovated in 1990, the National Park Inn shelters visitors to Mt. Rainier all year long.

National Park Inn

Mount Rainier Guest Services
P.O. Box 108
Ashford, WA 98304
(206) 569-2275

History

The sight must have been a surprising one, even for James Longmire, who considered himself an expert on Mt. Rainier.

Longmire had been exploring the mountain since bringing his family up the Oregon Trail thirty years earlier. In 1870, he had guided mountaineers Hazard Stevens and Philemon Van Trump to the base of Mt. Rainier, helping them to become the first Europeans to reach the summit.

On this day in 1883, Longmire was leading Van Trump and other climbers down the mountain. The party returned to their base camp and started looking around for the horses they had left there. Searching for the lost animals, Longmire found himself in an unusual place: a steamy, swampy meadow where hot water came bubbling out of the ground to fill strange, murky pools.

Longmire recognized these as mineral springs, and in their eerie vapors he smelled profit. (Famed naturalist John Muir would later describe Longmire as a "tall, wiry, enterprising money-maker.") Never revealing his discovery to the other mountaineers, Longmire snuck back several months later and staked his claim — twenty acres of land containing some fifty mineral springs. There the Longmire family started the first tourist accommodations on Mt. Rainier: a simple log cabin in 1884, then a two-story cedar plank hotel, just thirty feet long and twenty feet wide, in 1890.

With the help of his sons, his grandsons, and some local Indians, Longmire carved out a dirt road from the resort to the town of Yelm. The family also built bathhouses, sinking cedar tubs into the ground near the springs. Because local Indians claimed that the mineral waters had miraculous healing powers, the family called their resort "Longmire's Medical Springs."

Every summer for many years, James Longmire and his son Eclaine operated horse trains to bring guests to the mountain. For eight dollars a week, visitors could stay in the hotel and enjoy soaking in the hot tubs, or try other healthful luxuries like mud baths and "sulphur plunges." Upon request, the Longmires would lead their guests on hikes to the Paradise flower meadows, or up to the summit.

Together, the Longmires' hospitality and the area's natural beauty made Mt. Rainier into a popular vacation spot — maybe too popular. Campers were depleting the mountain's forests, chopping down the trees for firewood. Some visitors set fire to whole groves of fir trees to create pretty nighttime displays. In response, the National Geographic Society, the Sierra Club, and other organizations called for the mountain to be protected. Their cry was heard: Congress made Mt. Rainier America's fifth national park in 1899.

The news came too late to be heard by James Longmire; he had died two years earlier. Now operated by his children and grandchildren, the Longmire Springs Hotel was the center of a bustling community. But with success came competition. In 1906, the Milwaukee Railroad built a big, three-story hotel across the street. This new "National Park Inn" could sleep sixty guests — compared to the Longmires' twenty — and had a tent camp that slept seventy-five people.

Instead of rising to meet the challenge, the Longmire family quit the hotel business in 1916, a decision probably triggered by the death of Eclaine a year before. The resort's new management, however, did expand the resort, adding sixteen cottages and a new annex. The two-story, seventeen-room annex was a wood frame building, created in the simple, rustic style that had become a tradition in national parks across the country.

Now there were three hotels at Longmire, but not for long. That same year, all tourist accommodations in the park were turned over to the Rainier National Park Co. The new ownership made its own improvements, moving the annex across the street to sit next to the National Park

Inn and burning down the old Longmire Springs Hotel. In 1926 another fire, this one accidental, destroyed the National Park Inn, but left the annex unharmed. The only hotel left in Longmire, the annex assumed the name of its predecessor, and is now called the National Park Inn.

Over the years, the building has seen many changes: a kitchen wing added in 1926; a covered porch in 1968; a new roof in 1974. A major renovation was completed in 1990, expanding the inn from sixteen to twenty-five rooms by adding a new side wing. In spite of modernization inside, the outside structure is basically the same; many of the original timbers, placed in 1916, still support the inn.

The National Park Inn today

On the outside, the National Park Inn is an old-fashioned mountain lodge, with a shingled roof and a back porch. Inside it's more contemporary. All the rooms are decorated in the same light shades of yellow and pink, but they come in a variety of configurations: two single beds, a queen-size bed, two double beds; private bathroom, no private bathroom. "Old Hickory" furniture helps give the inn a rustic air.

Downstairs, the inn's lounge is a quiet, unassuming little room. Off to the side of the building, it's a cozy place to enjoy a card game or a good book while soaking up the heat from a unique river rock fireplace. Like the lounge, the inn's dining room is plain and pleasant. Dinners cost $10-15, featuring some of the fancy dishes so well-known at Paradise, and simpler, family-style fare like hamburgers and sandwiches.

What to do in Longmire

Take a tour of the buildings in Longmire. Most of them date back to the 1910s and 1920s; the **General Store** gift shop, for example, was constructed as a club house in 1911. Look around the **Longmire Museum**, built in 1916 as Mt. Rainier's first park headquarters. Many of the tiny museum's exhibits — including Native American baskets, stuffed animals, and historic photos — have been on display for over fifty years. All around Longmire, you'll find scenic **hiking and nature trails.** Park rangers present **campfire programs** at nearby Cougar Rock Campground on summer evenings. Although there are no rentals in the park, **horseback-riding** is allowed on some designated trails. **Fishing** is permitted in most lakes and streams.

Room Rates: Room without private bath $56, room with private bath $78, two-room unit with bath $105.

Restrictions: No smoking.

Reservations: A few weeks in advance for weekends.

Room Features: Most rooms have private baths. All come with coffee-makers and a supply of fresh coffee. No telephones or television sets.

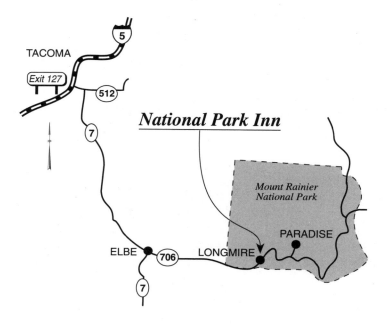

How to get there

From Interstate 5, take Exit 127, just south of Tacoma, onto Highway 512. After a few minutes, take Highway 7 south to Elbe. There switch onto Highway 706, which will take you into Mt. Rainier National Park. Then follow the signs to Longmire.

Paradise Inn

Mount Rainier Guest Services
P.O. Box 108
Ashford, WA 98304
(206) 569-2275

History

"Oh, it looks just like paradise!"

That was the cry of Eclaine Longmire's wife, Martha, when she first saw this valley. Its lush meadows, watered by glaciers and brimming with wildflowers, enchanted campers and picnickers at the turn of the century. Mountain climbers rested here, mustering their strength to conquer the summit of Mt. Rainier. Yet this wild Eden offered its pilgrims no shelter until, in 1916, the Rainier National Park Co. began construction on a mighty mountain lodge in the valley called Paradise.

Just below the valley, a forest had been ravaged by a recent fire. Beautiful Alaska cedar trees, killed by the fire and seasoned by time, had weathered to a fine silver gray. Now they were hauled by horses up to Paradise. Carved into great beams and rafters, they were set into place without the use of nails, often simply notched and joined log cabin-style.

The heart of the lodge was its lobby. More than 100 feet long, its cathedral-like ceiling fifty feet high, this giant hall was built of heavy wood posts, beams, and trusses, a massive stone fireplace guarding each end. Such an impressive room deserved equally impressive furnishings. The man who created them was Hans Fraehnke, an elderly German carpenter. In 1919, he spent a long, cold, lonely winter at the lodge. Working by lamplight, he carved all of the lobby's furniture by hand. Out of Fraehnke's

71

Against the backdrop of Mt. Rainier's summit, the Paradise Inn stands proudly, surrounded by lush meadowlands.

skill and the finest yellow cedar were born throne-like chairs, huge tables (one weighing more than 1,500 pounds), a thirteen-foot grandfather's clock, and an upright piano.

After its completion, hundreds of nature lovers flocked to the Paradise Inn each year — so many that an annex to the lodge, with 100 more rooms, had to be built in 1920. But during the Depression, general manager Paul Sceva had to come up with creative ways to keep the inn's rooms full. One of his favorite techniques for getting publicity was hosting celebrity guests.

72

Through the 1930s, Sceva "collected" Shirley Temple, Tyronne Power, Cecil B. De Mille, and the crown prince of Norway.

His most honored guest was a surprise. One day in June 1945, before the lodge had opened for the summer, Sceva found out that President Harry Truman was coming to Paradise — the next day. Sceva and his staff worked all night to clean the inn and prepare a formal luncheon. It must have been a success, because after lunch Truman thanked his hosts by playing a song for them on the lobby's rustic piano.

Sceva tried many other schemes to attract tourists. One year he built a nine-hole golf course in Paradise Valley. That failed to catch on and soon was abandoned. Then he brought an Eskimo and a dog sled team to Paradise to give rides, but the dogs cost so much to feed that Sceva had to sell them. Next, Sceva set up a motorcycle hill climb, but had to give up on this event, too — it caused too much damage to the hillside.

Sceva's real triumph was the Silver Ski Championship. First held in 1934, this 3.16-mile race for experts only attracted some 30,000 sports fans in its first year. Billed as "the wildest annual ski race on the North American continent," the championship brought Paradise national attention. A ski lift and ski trails were built. Olympic tryouts and national slalom championships were held there. Paradise had become the winter playground of the Northwest.

But with the coming of World War II, the Silver Ski race had to be canceled, and Paradise lost its status as a mecca for skiers. Wartime restrictions on rubber and gas discouraged people from driving to the mountains.

Business picked up again in peacetime, but the lodge was deteriorating. Every winter for decades, ten to twenty feet of snow had fallen on Paradise, causing the lodge's structure to bend under its weight and gradually pushing the building downhill. In the 1960s, the National Park Service proposed a plan to demolish Paradise Inn and build a more modern structure. All over the United States, millions of the lodge's past guests raised howls of protest. So instead of bulldozing the lodge, in 1979 the Park Service budgeted $1.75 million to restore it. They straightened the old lodge and gave it new walls and foundations. Exterior steel beams were used to prop up the building, but were covered in log "jackets" so they wouldn't mare the lodge's rustic appearance.

More recently, another restoration has taken place. With the golf courses and ski lifts long gone, the park service is repairing the flowered meadows around the lodge. Much as they did one hundred years ago, nature lovers are discovering the beauty of Paradise.

The Paradise Inn today

Rooms at Paradise Inn come in a variety of shapes, sizes, and degrees of tastefulness. Many in the original, front portion of the lodge are decorated in contemporary pastel colors, with futon couches and wood beams passing through white walls. But the majority of rooms, those in the back annex, haven't been redecorated since the 1960s, and it shows. Their generic wood paneling and lime-green carpets make them feel dark and cheap. Still, all the rooms here are comfortable, especially with the big, fluffy comforters on the beds.

In any event, you won't want to hang around your room — not with the magnificent lobby just down the hall. Everything here is either large or extra-large, from the cedar log pillars to Hans Fraehnke's mammoth furniture. Yet the hall has its subtle charms as well. Scandinavian designs are painted on the woodwork in bright blues and oranges, and each of the hanging lanterns is decorated with the design of a different wildflower found at Paradise. Everyone seems to relax here: Hikers, climbers, and tourists gather in front of the fire, the huge proportions of the room absorbing their conversations with ease.

The inn's dining room has much the same look as the lobby, and almost its size. Dinner entrees ($12-20) include seafood, pasta, and steak. The dining room serves three meals a day, but is best known for one meal a week — the Sunday brunch, a feast of pastries, fruits, and cheeses.

What to do in Paradise

The spectacular **scenery** and **wildlife** at Paradise draws visitors from all over the world. Many favorite **trails** are found near the lodge, including the Nisqually Vista trail, the Skyline Trail, and the Wonderland Trail. At the **visitor center** nearby, you can see free exhibits on animals, glaciers, geography, wildflowers, and mountain-climbing. Park service employees lead **nature walks** and other programs. **Climbing** instruction is available from Rainier Mountaineering, Inc.

Room Rates: Room without private bath $60, room with bath $85, two-room unit with bath $109, suite with sitting room $115.

Reservations: Call two to four months in advance.

Restrictions: No smoking allowed.

Room Features: Some with private bath. No telephones or television sets.

Open: Mid-May to early October.

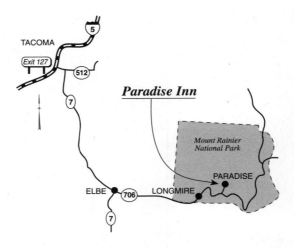

How to get there
From Interstate 5, take Exit 127, just south of Tacoma, onto Highway 512. After a few minutes, take Highway 7 south to Elbe. There switch onto Highway 706, which will take you into Mt. Rainier National Park. Then follow the signs to Paradise.

**In the 1880s, Elizabeth and William Kindred opened their two-story
farmhouse to visitors who came to enjoy Tokeland's ocean beaches.**

Tokeland Hotel

100 Hotel Road
Tokeland, WA 98590
(206) 267-7006

History

When George Brown paddled an Indian dugout canoe across Shoalwater Bay in 1858 and got out on a long, low finger of land, he didn't plan to stay.

Brown had come a long way, leaving Philadelphia in1849 to search for gold in California, run a butcher shop in Portland, then travel up the Pacific Coast. He planned to follow the fur traders' trail north and start a farm in Chehalis County. Yet on that point of land along the Washington Coast, Brown found fish, ducks, geese, and game, as well as beaches full of clams, crabs, and oysters. The place was called Toke Point, after Chief Toke of the Shoalwater Indians, who used it as a summer home. Brown decided to settle there as well. He later wrote to his relatives: "I said to myself, 'Well, George, I don't see anything better than this place, so will just pitch my tent and establish a little home.'"

Once George had built his "little home," he sent for his wife, Charlotte, and young son, Albert. The family was settled into its new home by the winter of 1859. Three years later, Charlotte had to be paddled hurriedly across the bay to Bruceport; a midwife was found in time to help her deliver a daughter, Elizabeth.

"Lizzie" had a happy childhood, growing up on her parents' farm and playing with the Indian children. When she was eighteen, she met a young carpenter from Portland named William Kindred. In November of 1880, they were married, and the young couple purchased a share of Lizzie's parents' property to start their own farm. Their large, two-story farmhouse was completed in 1885.

Changes were taking place on Toke's Point. Tourists had discovered its beaches, but when they arrived, there was no hotel to house them. So Lizzie provided visitors with food and lodging in the Kindred home. The "Kindred Inn" was so successful that in 1899 William built an addition to the house.

The Tokeland Hotel (as the Kindred Inn was renamed in 1910) became famous for its fine food, especially the fresh seafood right off the beach and fresh produce from the Kindreds' garden. Two steamers, the "Shamrock" and the "Reliable," brought in visitors who had taken the train to South Bend. William would meet the boats at the dock at the end of Toke's Point, and drive the guests to the hotel in a horse-drawn carriage called a "tally-ho." Visitors came from as far away as Idaho and Southern California to enjoy the Kindreds' hospitality. They admired the hotel's unique lobby, which Lizzie had decorated with all the Indian baskets, mats, and beadwork she had been given during a lifetime of friendship with the local tribes.

Lizzie was a friend not only to the local Indians, but also to Chinese immigrants in the area. Chinese laborers had been used to build the railroads, but now that the lines were finished, many of the workers became victims of racial hatred. Lizzie helped them escape by hiding them in a space behind the hotel's fireplace. (Ask someone on the hotel's staff to show you the hiding place.) Once the coast was clear, the immigrants would be smuggled onto ships heading north, where they could find safe passage back to Asia. One Chinese man, nicknamed "Charley," died while hidden behind the fireplace. Rumor has it that his spirit still haunts the building, and has appeared as a small cloud floating across the hallway. Current owners say "Charley" is a benevolent spirit who has protected the Tokeland Hotel, perhaps out of gratitude to the memory of Lizzie Kindred.

As Lizzie and William Kindred grew older, their daughter Maude helped them run the hotel. Maude had dreams of promoting Tokeland as a West Coast "Coney Island." With her parent's permission, she remodeled the interior of the hotel and added several new attractions: a golf course and club house; a gun club; a general store; even a riding club with stables and bridal trails. Maude's dreams were cut short, however. The coming of the Great Depression brought an end to much of the hotel's prosperity. In

1932, a hurricane destroyed most of the resort's new facilities.

The hotel was left intact, but the Kindred family didn't watch over it for much longer. Lizzie Kindred died in 1931, shortly after celebrating her Golden Wedding Anniversary. Her daughter Maude died eight years later, followed by Lizzie's other daughter, Bess. The only member of the family left, William died in 1943 at age eighty-six. He left the hotel to his housekeeper (that decision raised a few eyebrows). She sold it to the Nelson Crab and Oyster Company, which tried to use it first as a boarding house for its employees, then as a hotel and dining room. Both attempts failed — the hotel closed in 1949.

The Tokeland Hotel came back to life when it was purchased by another family. Dave and Emily Hawthorne reopened the hotel in the summer of 1950, and Emily's parents remodeled the old clubhouse to make it into a licensed tavern with a pool table. Every summer for twenty years, the Hawthornes and their five children welcomed guests to the Tokeland Hotel. Local people lined up for the Hawthornes' famous Sunday dinners, and passed the time with dances and drunken brawls in the Capt's Tavern.

Throughout the 1970s and 1980s, several different families ran the hotel, none of them with much success. After failing as a dinner theater, the hotel sat vacant for several years. The ceilings became black with mold; blackberry vines grew up over the walls and crept in through the windows; weeds took over the overgrown lawns. It seems fitting that another family would rescue the Tokeland. Scott and Katherine White bought the Tokeland in December of 1989 and embarked on a frantic five-month renovation, opening the hotel in time for Mother's Day of 1990.

The Tokeland Hotel today

Staying in the Tokeland Hotel, you feel as if you've come home to your grandmother's farmhouse in the country. The nineteen guest rooms have an old-fashioned coziness that you rarely find anywhere. All of the furniture is antique, much of it going back to the time of the Kindreds: Room 1 holds the Kindreds' bridal bed, while the child-size Room ½ is furnished with a tiny dresser built for Lizzie when she was eight. Bathrooms are strictly "down the hall," but even these are light and pretty, stenciled with seahorses and seashells.

The atmosphere here is quiet and deliciously reclusive. Beds squeak;

floors creak; a roaring fire pops and crackles in the big brick fireplace downstairs. The comfortable sitting room is decorated with strange odds and ends of Americana: logging saws, old-time radios, a brass bed warmer. On stormy nights, it's the perfect place to share a jigsaw puzzle or nestle down with a good book. If the weather's clear the next morning, you may want to play horseshoes, volleyball, or croquet on the sweeping green lawns out back.

As in times past, the Tokeland Hotel is well-known locally for its solid, home-cooked meals. Reasonably priced dinners ($8-10) feature fresh local ingredients, like crab and oysters. Every Sunday evening in the plain, homey dining room, the hotel's staff proudly serves its specialty, a cranberry potroast so tender each bite seems to dissolve on your tongue.

What to do around Tokeland

Tokeland's not much of a town; it's more like a cluster of beach houses and a few shops. The hotel's isolated location makes it a peaceful retreat, where you can enjoy quiet activities like **kite-flying, bird-watching, bicycling, clam-digging,** and **crabbing. Beach** access is right across the street, so you can enjoy sunning on a strip of white sand or wander the miles of mud flats that appear when the tide goes out. Better beaches dot the coast to the north on the way to **Westport,** a lively resort town a half hour's drive away.

Room Rates: $65 for two people, $55 for one person. Includes full breakfast.

Restrictions: No smoking in guest rooms or upstairs hallways. Children and well-behaved pets are welcome, but pets cannot be left alone in rooms.

Reservations: Necessary during the summer, often not needed in the winter.

Room Features: No private baths, no television sets, no telephones.

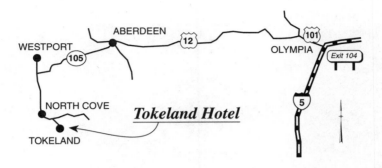

How to get there

From Interstate 5, take Exit 104 near Olympia. Drive west on Highway 101, then west on State Route 12 (also called State Route 8) to Aberdeen. There take the Westport exit, heading first west, then south on Highway 105. After you pass North Cove, take the Tokeland exit and continue for two miles. The hotel will be a large grey building on your left.

Twin lanterns light up the face of the Shelburne Inn, one of the oldest hostelries in Washington state.

Shelburne Inn

4415 Pacific Way
Seaview, WA 98644
(206) 642-2442

History

Jonathan Stout was a man with vision, but sometimes it takes more than one lifetime for a vision to be realized.

Arriving in the oceanside town of Unity (now called Ilwaco) in 1859, Stout was a cooper, or barrel-maker, by trade. During his life on the peninsula, he also became a justice of the peace, a saloon-keeper, a postmaster, a farmer, and the owner of his own stagecoach line, "the Lightning Express."

As if that wasn't enough, Stout founded his own town. He had noticed that every summer Portland families came to camp on the beach. So in 1881, Stout bought 153 acres of land along the ocean, divided it into lots, then sold the lots for $75-200 apiece to families who wanted to build beach cottages. Stout had trouble naming the new resort town, however. He first called it "Stout's," then "Ocean View," then "North Pacific Beach." The name that finally stuck was "Seaview."

At the center of town, Stout built the Seaview Hotel. When the hotel was successful enough to be enlarged, Stout hired a young contractor, Charlie Beaver, to do the job. Beaver fell in love with Stout's daughter, Inez, while working on the hotel. The young couple were married in 1891.

Stout's lifetime of good fortune was running out, though. His beautiful hotel burned to the ground in 1892, leaving him financially ruined. He died three years later. His daughter and son-in-law, however, used property they inherited from him to build their own hotel in 1896. Charlie Beaver named the two-story wooden hotel after a hotel in Ireland that he had read about in a novel, the Shelburne Hotel.

The Beavers ran the hotel until 1906, when Charlie Beaver took a job in Portland and the family moved there. The new owner, William Hoare, later bought some land nearby where two houses stood. Hoare hired a team of horses to pull the Shelburne Hotel across the street onto his new property. Covered passages were built, connecting the three to make one large building. Later one of the two houses was torn down or burned, leaving the Shelburne Hotel as it appears today.

During the thirty years that the Hoare family operated the hotel, it was almost always full — a boarding house for teachers in the winter, a vacation resort in the summer. In those days vacations tended to last longer. Women and their children would come to the Shelburne to spend several weeks at the beach. The men would come for the weekends, arriving on Friday night aboard the "Papa train."

Many stories remain from the days when the Hoares ran the Shelburne. Local man Jack Williams loved telling his favorite tale: one day he was kissing young Julia Hoare on the feinting couch under the stairs (the couch that is still there today) when her father came running down the stairs with a shotgun. Williams proposed on the spot, and the two were married soon after. Apparently it worked out: Jack and Julia Williams spent the next thirty-five years running local movie theaters.

Art Nouveau stained-glass windows discovered in a church in England, decorate this classy dining room.

After the Hoare family sold it in 1946, the hotel passed through the hands of two other families. In 1977, it was bought by a young married couple, David Campiche and Laurie Anderson. They embarked on a long-term renovation of the then run-down hotel. Originally in the antique business, the couple at first made ends meet by selling antiques in the hotel. Guest would stay in the hotel and, if any of the furnishings caught their eye, buy them and take them home. Those penny-pinching days are long past, however. Today the Shelburne Inn is one of the Northwest's most popular hostelries, and is recognized as the oldest continually operating hotel in Washington state.

The Shelburne Inn today

This brightly colored inn with its Art Nouveau stained-glass windows has all the most elegant elements of the Victorian Age: ruffled curtains, marble-topped dressers, fine rugs, ornate wooden wardrobes. A few eclectic touches, such as patchwork quilts and contemporary art prints, do well to lighten the tone a bit. I wouldn't recommend the three least expensive rooms; these are a bit plain and cramped. For slightly more you'll get a larger room that's truly stunning.

The lobby downstairs is an odd conglomeration of dining room, sitting room, and gift shop. Somehow, with its big brick fireplace, deep leather sofa, and brass bed-warmer on the wall, it works. Take a close look at the front desk, originally a wooden altar in a local Episcopal Church.

Under the same roof but different management, the Shoalwater Restaurant has earned a national reputation. This attractive, quiet, unassuming dining room produces beautifully prepared dishes such as roast rabbit sirloin, Chinook salmon, or sautéed oysters for $15-30. Equally magnificent are the Shelburne Inn breakfasts that come with your room. Guests choose from such fare as stuffed French toast with cranberry sauce, scrambled eggs with smoked salmon, and razor clam fritters.

What to do around Seaview

The **ocean beaches** are beautiful, but before you go swimming, ask around — there's a strong undertow in many places. **Sport fishing** is highly popular. You can learn more about the area's history in the **Ilwaco Heritage Museum**. A short drive north will take you to the busy resort town of **Long Beach** or to the historic settlement of **Oysterville**. To the south, you can explore **Fort Canby State Park**, where there are **hiking** and **picnicking** facilities, two **lighthouses**, and the **Lewis and Clark Interpretive Center**.

Room Rates: Rooms $89-125, suites $160.

Reservations: Call one month in advance for summer and weekends, earlier for August. There is a two-night minimum for most weekends.

Restrictions: No smoking, no pets. Quiet, well-behaved children welcome.

Room Features: Private bathrooms, no television sets or telephones.

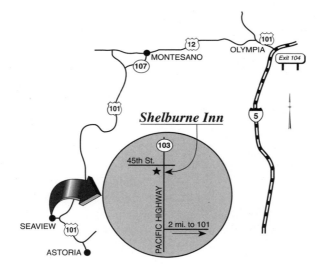

How to get there

From Seattle, take Interstate 5 to Olympia, then take Exit 104 and head west on Highway 101, then west on State Route 12. When you reach Montesano, take Highway 107 south, then Highway 101 south all the way to Seaview. From Portland, take Highway 30 north to Astoria. Cross the Columbia River on the Astoria Bridge, then take Highway 101 north. When you reach Seaview, turn right onto Pacific Highway 103. The inn will be on your left, on the corner of the highway and 45th Street.

Oregon

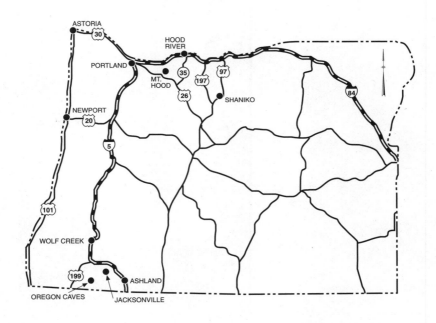

CHRISTINE UMMEL

Wealthy banker Frank Patton built this white neoclassical mansion on a hill overlooking Astoria in 1902.

Rosebriar Hotel

636 Fourteenth Street
Astoria, OR 97103
(503) 325-7427 / (800) 487-0224

History

Of all the cities in the Northwest, Astoria has the longest and perhaps the richest history. Captain Robert Gray first saw this site in 1792 when he discovered the mouth of the Columbia River. The Lewis and Clark Expedition spent the winter only a few miles away. John Jacob Astor's Pacific Fur Co. set up business here in 1811, making it the United States' oldest settlement west of the Rockies.

One of Astoria's founding families was the Welches, who arrived by wagon train from Ohio in 1844. James and Nancy Welch bought a large tract of land, built a log cabin, and started a farm. Their daughter Sarah was the first white child born in the area.

Fifty-five years later, the Welches' land was split between two other prominent families. In 1901, Capt. James Flavel, head of Astoria's richest and most powerful family, built his mansion on the site of the Welches' cabin. Next door, where the Welches' garden may have grown, wealthy banker Frank Patton built his house the following year.

Flavel and Patton were rivals and often argued about where the line between their properties should be drawn. It was common knowledge that Patton intended his house to compete in size and style with Flavel's. Patton's white mansion had a neoclassical design, prim and orderly with its square corners and perfect proportions. At each corner of the house was a fluted pillar; nine more pillars supported the front porch. Inside, the house's woodwork was hand-carved in red fir. Shields and circling vines decorated the plaster ceilings. Downstairs, the foyer was wallpapered in Pompeii red and stenciled in gold leaf.

Looking down on the city from his house on the hill, Patton did well in Astoria's high society. He became president of the Astoria Savings Bank and served as a port commissioner. The Pattons were one of the first families in town to have electricity, telephone service, and an automobile. Then, sometime between 1925 and 1930, Patton's wife, Maud, died. Soon afterward, Patton did something that obliterated his social status: he married his live-in housekeeper, Hazel, and adopted her children. Local aristocrats were shocked by such disgraceful behavior. The "new" Mrs. Patton tried not to let the town gossip upset her and soon began to redecorate the mansion, but she was never accepted into Astorian society.

Not much is known about Frank Patton's later life. One rumor claims that he lost most of his money in the 1929 stock market crash. In 1948, Frank Patton died at age eighty-six. His wife sold the house and moved away that same year.

The new owners were the Sisters of Holy Names, an order of Catholic nuns who taught at the Star of the Sea School across the street. To convert the house into a convent, Portland architect Francis Jacoberger built an addition that doubled the size of the building. The extension was so flawlessly done that it's hard to tell where the old building ends and the new one begins. A chapel was constructed on the first floor, complete with stained glass windows, an altar, and two confessionals. (Today the chapel is used as a conference room and furnished with a piano that the sisters used to give their students music lessons.)

The Sisters of Holy Names lived in their new convent for more than twenty years, so it must have served their needs well (though local legend has it that the nuns, like the Patton family, had fierce arguments with their neighbors, the Flavels). In 1973, the convent closed. The Archdiocese rented the building to the state of Oregon, which used it for nine years as the Phoenix House, a home for troubled teenage girls. One year the building served as a housing and training center for mentally disabled adults.

Those ten years took a harsh toll on the building; woodwork was destroyed and flimsy walls constructed to make room for more residents. In 1983, two sisters bought the building and turned it into the "Rosebriar

Inn," Astoria's first bed-and-breakfast. Nine years later, however, the building had again fallen into disrepair. It was purchased by Stephen and Claudia Tuckman, who completed an extensive renovation and opened the "Rosebriar Hotel" in June of 1993. Though it narrowly missed being placed on the National Historic Register, the Rosebriar Hotel has been made an Astoria Historic Landmark and is valued as a tribute to the city's colorful past.

CHRISTINE UMMEL

The Sisters of Holy Names created this folk art shrine in the 1950s, when the mansion was used as a convent.

The Rosebriar Hotel today

This small, neoclassical hotel is blessed by an air of quiet graceful-ness, decorated in soothing shades of ivory and olive, mahogany and rose. The sophisticated masculinity of the rooms, manifested in maroon wing-back chairs and high-backed wooden beds, is offset by feminine touches like the rose-patterned comforters and satiny dust ruffles. The ten rooms all have a similar decor, but come in a variety of sizes and features. Families and honeymooners enjoy staying in the 1885 Carriage House in back, which has its own fireplace, spa, and kitchenette.

In the hotel's formal lobby, you can relax amid long draperies and flowered sofas. A rare antique piano of burled myrtle wood stands in one corner, brought from Dresden, Germany in the late nineteenth century. Every morning, a light breakfast is served in the small dining room, featuring unique dishes — hash brown quiche, salmon fritata, or Finnish pancakes with hot apples. The grounds around the hotel are also pleasant. In the side yard, look for a folk art shrine the Sisters of Holy Names built in 1952 to house a statue of the Virgin Mary.

What to do in Astoria

This small waterfront city is filled with **shops, cafes, galleries**, and **museums**. It's well known for its **Victorian homes**; one favorite example is the 1885 **Flavel House**, the family's other mansion, now a museum. The city's naval history is on display at the **Columbia River Maritime Museum**, with the lightship *Columbia* moored outside. Nearby, you can visit a replica of Lewis and Clark's camp at **Fort Clatsop National Memorial**. In large **Fort Stevens State Park**, there is a military museum, picnic and camping facilities, nature trails, boating, biking, and miles of ocean beaches.

Room Rates: Rooms $50-100, carriage house $130. Breakfast included. Lower rates available during the off-season.

Reservations: Always recommended, but not always necessary.

Restrictions: No smoking, no pets, well-mannered children welcome.

Room Features: Private baths, television sets, telephones.

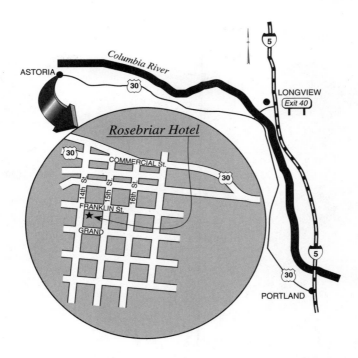

How to get there

From Interstate 5, take Exit 40 at Longview. Use Highway 433 to cross the Columbia River, then head west on Highway 30. As you enter downtown Astoria, take a left onto Fourteenth Street and drive three blocks up the hill. The Rosebriar Hotel will be on your left, at the corner of Fourteenth and Franklin.

This stately mansion, with its tall Greek columns and classical portico, is named for its resemblance to the home of the president.

Portland's White House

1914 NE 22nd Avenue
Portland, OR 97212
(503) 287-7131

History

Many Northwest mansions have a rags-to-riches story in their pasts. Portland's White House has two.

The first begins in 1889. The Lytle brothers, Robert and Joseph, came west from Wisconsin and started a grocery store in the logging community of Grays Harbor, Washington. After a few years, one of their regular customers was unable to pay the bills he had run up. He gave them his small logging company in lieu of payment. With some hard work and remarkably good luck, the Lytle Co. became one of the largest logging operations in the area. The brothers both built mansions side by side in Hoquiam. (Today Robert's house, called the Hoquiam Castle, is open for tours, and Joseph's is a bed-and-breakfast.) Eventually, Robert Lytle decided to move his family away from the rough-and-tumble logging town to a more civilized environment. His choice: a classy neighborhood in Portland, Oregon.

For his second home, Lytle hired respected architect David Lochead Williams to build a mansion in the Southern Federalist style. As the story goes, when Lytle's wife Ida was about ten years old, she had visited an aunt who lived in an old plantation manor in Virginia. Ida Lytle had always wanted a house like that, and now she got her wish. The mansion's stately Greek columns, twenty-five feet high, supported a classical portico. Inside, the large entrance hall was paneled in Honduran mahogany, floored in

95

solid oak, and trimmed in gold. Crystal chandeliers hung from the ceiling; hand-painted French wallpaper covered the walls. An elegant double staircase folded in on itself, alongside windows of brilliant stained glass.

The regal white mansion, completed in 1912 at the astonishingly high price of $46,000, soon became a favorite gathering place for Portland society. The Lytles held afternoon teas, receptions, formal dinners, even dances in their basement ballroom. Sadly, Robert Lytle only enjoyed his mansion for about four years. He died in 1916 at age sixty. His widow and daughter moved away. According to one report, Ida Lytle ended up in the Midwest, where she supposedly spent the family fortune, then met another millionaire and married him.

Our second rags-to-riches story involves the Hawley family, who bought the house about five years later. At age seventeen, Willard P. Hawley had taken a job at a local paper mill. For a dollar a day, he hauled wood and loaded it into the mill's boilers on a twelve-hour shift, from noon to midnight. After six months, he was put in charge of a paper-making machine. One boss caught him working to improve the efficiency of the machine, and promoted him to superintendent of the mill. Hawley kept working his way up until, in 1908, he started his own corporation, the Hawley Pulp & Paper Co. in Oregon City. By 1921, he was one of the wealthiest men in the region, and lived in the Lytle mansion.

Like the Lytles, the Hawleys were great entertainers. Their tastes were more musical, however, and the family invited many popular singers and musicians to perform in their home. These concerts were broadcast by the Hawleys' private radio station, which Hawley and his oldest son, Willard Jr., founded in their basement. According to one newspaper account, the Hawleys had one of the first licensed radio stations in Oregon.

When the Hawleys grew tired of their hobby, they put the radio station up for sale. Several students from Benson Polytechnical School saw the sign "FOR SALE — RADIO STATION" in a store window, and asked their principal if they could use their student body funds to purchase it. The station, now KBPS for the school's name, went on the air March 23, 1923, and has broadcast from the school ever since.

Meanwhile, the Hawleys soon were to become even more well-known in Portland. They were the subject of much local gossip when Willard Hawley Jr. divorced his young wife, Marjorie, because she allegedly

96

deserted him. Hawley Jr. moved back into his parents' mansion, bringing his daughter, Adele, to be raised by her grandparents.

It was Adele Hawley who sold the mansion, moving away from Portland to marry an Air Force pilot in 1940. Since then, the mansion has had a variety of owners, including banker Harvey Dick, known for renovating Portland's Hoyt Hotel in the 1960s. Another owner wanted to turn the mansion into a wedding chapel, but her neighbors objected. She was so angry that she painted the house pink, and sold most of the grounds to a real-estate developer, who built an apartment complex.

Over forty-five years, the mansion deteriorated. Ceilings fell in, walls rotted out, the banisters and stained glass windows came loose. When Mary Mozen-Hough and her husband Larry Hough bought the house in 1984, they counted forty-three leaks in the roof. Renovating it one room at a time, they restored much of the mansion's original grandeur. Now listed on the National Register of Historic Places, the house is known as Portland's White House because of its uncanny resemblance to another elegant mansion — the one in Washington, D.C.

Portland's White House today

You simply can't get more romantic than this. Six guest rooms have been lovingly decorated with lace curtains, floral wallpaper, and beautiful wooden antiques. In the Baron's Room, you'll find a four-poster bed with pink canopy, Persian rugs, and a mirrored wardrobe inlaid with carvings of seashells. The old-fashioned Balcony Room is dressed all in blue and white with an ornate brass bed, while the serene Garden Room has its own deck, overlooking a waterfall, fishpond, and rose-covered wall. Even the bathrooms are charming: five of them are furnished with claw-foot bathtubs original to the house.

Downstairs, the parlor is a vision of Victorian elegance, its French windows draped in white lace and armchairs covered in velvet. Afternoon tea is served in the little library next door. In the formal dining room, lavishly decorated in mahogany and crystal, guests gather around a long lace-covered table for a rich breakfast, often eggs benedict. The basement — a ballroom once more, now with a checkered floor and mirrored walls — is a favorite setting for weddings and receptions.

CHRISTINE UMMEL

You simply can't get more romantic than this. The Baron's Room has a four-poster canopy bed, Persian rugs, and a mirrored wardrobe.

What to do in Portland

The White House is only a few minutes' drive from **downtown Portland**, and there's plenty to do in the immediate area as well. Close to the White House are the **Oregon Convention Center**, popular shopping mall **Lloyd Center**, and **Memorial Coliseum**. Farther south is the **Oregon Museum of Science and Industry**. **Washington Park**, in southwest Portland, is home to rose gardens, Japanese gardens, a forestry museum, and a zoo. Less developed is the 1,000-acre **Forest Park**, the city's own nature preserve to the north. Architecture fans won't want to miss touring **Pittock Mansion**, built by a wealthy contemporary and rival of Robert Lytle, and the campus of **Reed College**.

Room Rates: $99-115. Breakfast included.

Reservations: Call a few months in advance, especially for summer weekends.

Restrictions: Children under twelve discouraged. No pets, no smoking.

Room Features: No television sets. All rooms have private bathrooms, clock radios, and telephones.

Portland's White House

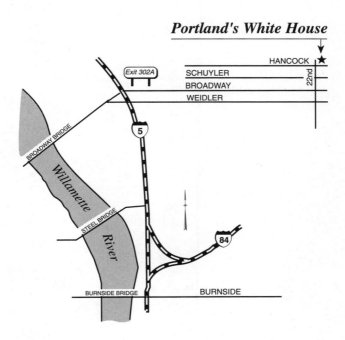

How to get there

In Portland, take Exit 302A off Interstate 5 and head east on Weidler Street. Drive for about twenty blocks, then turn left onto 22nd Avenue. The house will be on your right, at the corner of 22nd and Hancock.

Millionaire Simon Benson spent $1 million to build this luxurious downtown hotel in his beloved city of Portland.

Benson Hotel

309 SW Broadway
Portland, OR 97205
(503) 228-2000

History

When Simon Benson walked the streets of Portland, he didn't see the cosmopolitan center that we see today — the theaters, art museums, parks, and grand hotels. Instead, Benson saw a city that needed a strong dose of culture.

Unlike most people, Benson had enough money to give his favorite city an injection of class. Originally from Norway, in 1867 his family had immigrated first to New York, then to Wisconsin. Sixteen-year-old Simon worked as a farm laborer and taught himself to speak English. After spending several years in logging camps, he brought his wife and baby son to the tall timbers of Oregon. Benson saved $800 in one year and used it to buy 160 acres of woodland. Over the next thirty years, the Benson Timber Co. would grow into a vast logging empire, making Benson a millionaire.

At age sixty, Benson was tired of making money and ready to spend it. "I wanted the fun of spending my money for the public good while I was still alive," he said. So Benson spent $100,000 to build the Benson Polytechnical School and gave $10,000 in loans to deserving students. Another $10,000 went to build twenty bronze quadruple-headed water fountains in downtown Portland. Given a choice, Benson believed, workmen would choose to drink water for free instead of buying a beer in the nearest tavern, thus living more virtuous lives (and having fewer Monday-morning hangovers to slow down logging operations).

To compete with other West Coast cities, Benson decided, Portland needed a luxury hotel. In 1911, he hired prominent local architect Albert Doyle to build a magnificent twelve-story hotel. (In his life, Doyle also designed the Multnomah County Library, the Multnomah Falls Lodge, parts of Reed College, and Benson's drinking fountains.) For Benson's hotel, Doyle imitated the famous Blackstone Hotel on Chicago's lakefront, creating a square brick tower with white terra cotta trim and a copper-colored mansard roof in the French Renaissance style.

No expense was too great. Benson had the walls of the lobby paneled in rare Circassian walnut (now extinct), brought in from Imperial Russia. White marble veined with gold was imported from Italy for the floors, and crystal chandeliers from Austria were hung from the ceiling. The white plaster ceilings were delicately carved, spread overhead like a huge lace canopy. It was the first public building in Portland to have elevators, and the first hotel in town with a private bathroom for each room. Total cost: $1 million.

Yet in spite of its grandeur, Benson's 160-room hotel was only considered an "annex" when it opened on March 5, 1913. Called the "New Oregon Hotel," it was joined to the older Oregon Hotel next door. (Many guest rooms still have the letters "OH" inlaid in holly wood on the oak doors.) Benson leased the building to the managers of the Oregon Hotel, but when the hotel lost money steadily over the first sixteen months, he took it back and managed it himself. After proving that it could be run profitably, Benson sold the hotel in 1919. The new owners ran it successfully until 1944, when its management was taken over by a fledgling hotel chain called Western (now Westin) Hotels.

In 1959, the "Westin Benson" was doing well, but the old Oregon Hotel had closed and become an eyesore. The three local families that owned the property bulldozed the older building, erecting a new tower of the Westin Benson in its place. The original tower was modernized, losing much of its classical style. When West Coast Grand Hotels bought the entire property in 1988, they renamed it "the Benson" and spent $17 million to restore the hotel's original 1913 appearance.

Through its history, the Benson has earned one record that few hotels can match: every U.S. president since Dwight D. Eisenhower (that's nine of them) has stayed here. When President Bill Clinton came to Portland for the Timber Summit on April 2, 1993, he stayed at the Benson. With him came Vice President Al Gore, four cabinet secretaries, eighty Secret Service agents, and 250 police officers. Security officers were stationed on the roof, and dump trucks loaded with gravel were parked alongside the hotel, to prevent someone from driving into the building with a car bomb. The president and his staff occupied a total of 150 rooms, the top five floors of the hotel. The next morning they all packed up and left, and by evening the Benson's rooms were full again.

The Benson today

Stepping into the Benson's lobby from the busy Portland streets, you feel like Cinderella arriving for her first night at the ball. Above you, chandeliers gleem with gold and crystal; pillars of polished wood surround you, radiating a golden glow; marble floors glint and shimmer beneath your feet. Around you, old friends meet for coffee and quiet conversation, while in the background a grand piano is played tenderly by knowing hands. You have been transported back in time to an era of elegance and extravagance.

Upstairs, the guest rooms, though hardly as opulent, are decorated in the same classic styling. They have a sophisticated, masculine air, tailored in tan and maroon, dark blues and light greys. The wood furnishings were designed to recall the graceful lines of the 1910s. Large windows, hung with meticulously folded striped curtains, look out on glittering night views of the lights of downtown Portland.

Over the decades, generations of Portlanders have come to the Benson to celebrate their special occasions. The hotel's fabulous halls have seen more than 4,000 wedding receptions. (Benson himself got married at the Benson, remarrying in 1920 at age sixty-eight.) The most romantic of these halls, the Crystal Ballroom, is decked with 7½-foot teardrop chandeliers and gold filligree trim scrolled along the white walls and ceiling. For special dinners, visitors can sample delicacies such as sautéed young rabbit or Cornish game hen in the London Grill, or enjoy a less formal, more exotic meal in the Polynesian-style Trader Vic's. One of the hotel's more recent additions is a modern exercise room.

What to do in downtown Portland

Contrary to Benson's 1911 opinion, the city of Portland is overflowing with entertainment and the arts. To name just a few attractions, there's the **Portland Art Museum**, the **Portland Saturday Market**, and **Waterfront Park**. Performing arts include the **Oregon Symphony Orchestra, Portland Opera, Oregon Ballet Theater, Portland Repertory Theater,** and **the Oregon Shakespeare Festival—Portland**. One of the city's more unusual museums is the **American Advertising Museum**, housed in the 1895 Erickson Saloon. History fans will want to look through the **Oregon Historical Center Museum**, or tour one of the city's many historic districts: the town's original commercial center in the **Skidmore district**, the High Victorian Italianate structures in the **Yamhill district**, and the homes of turn-of-the-century Asian immigrants in the **Chinatown district**.

Room Rates: Standard $130-165, deluxe $140-190, junior suites $155-205, penthouse suite $325, grand suite $600.

Restrictions: Children and pets are permitted. Both smoking and non-smoking floors are available.

Reservations: Always recommended.

Room Features: Private bathrooms. Two telephones with business/office features in each room. Television sets with on-command movies.

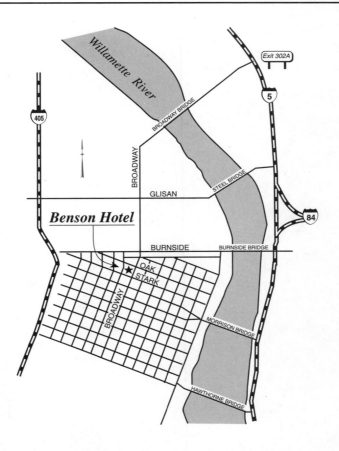

How to get there

From Interstate 5, take Exit 302A and cross the Willamette River on the Broadway Bridge. On the other side, keep to the left, following Broadway Avenue. The Benson will be on your right, between Oak Street and Stark Street.

COURTESY OF MCDONALD, BABB & CLARKSON, INC.

Framed by river and mountain, the face of this 1921 resort hotel looks out over the Columbia Gorge.

Columbia Gorge Hotel

4000 Westcliff Drive
Hood River, OR 97031
(503) 386-5566

History

If you've read about the Benson Hotel, you already know about Simon Benson — how the young Norwegian immigrant founded a vast logging empire, and used much of his wealth to beautify the city of Portland. But that's just part of the story.

Benson's visionary philanthropy didn't stop at the Portland city limits. He looked east, to the Columbia River Gorge, in his opinion one of the most beautiful places in America. Tourists, however, had no easy way to get there. Their newfangled automobiles could not withstand the bumpy dirt roads.

So Benson embarked on a new project: the creation of modern roads throughout Oregon, especially between Portland and the Columbia River Gorge. Thanks to Benson's influence in local politics — and some substantial help from his bank account — the scenic Columbia River Highway was built. It stretched 180 miles from Astoria to the town of Hood River. Completed in 1915, the highway was designed to complement the natural beauty of the Gorge; the sides of bridges were covered with indigenous stone, for example, to help them blend in with the terrain. Along the road, Benson bought attractive sites, like Multnomah Falls, to be used as roadside parks.

Once tourists could reach the Columbia Gorge, Benson wanted to provide them with a luxurious place to stay. He found the perfect location for his new hotel on a rocky bluff overlooking the gorge, with Mt. Hood in the background. Nearby, Phelps Creek cascaded off a 200-foot cliff to form a delicate waterfall called Wah-Gwin-Gwin (a Native American phrase meaning "rushing waters"). It was the site of the Wah Gwin Gwin Hotel, built in 1904 by Hood River pioneer Robert Rand. Benson tore down the little ma-and-pop hotel, leaving only the extensive gardens to surround his new "Waldorf of the West."

It looked like an Italian villa on the Mediterranean, with cream-colored stucco walls and a tower 100 feet high. The red tile roofs were taken from the Spanish mission style popular in California. A three-story hotel with forty-eight rooms, it cost over $400,000 and was completed in less than a year.

For the hotel's opening on June 18, 1921, hundreds of Portlanders drove through a downpour to get a grand tour and to shake hands with the famous Simon Benson. They also met master chef Henri Thiele, under whose care the Columbia Gorge Hotel became well-known for its fine cuisine. Prices were steep (seventy-five cents for a complete dinner) but the hotel soon attracted everyone from local townsfolk to U.S. presidents, and was a favorite hideaway for such Hollywood idols as Clara Bow, Myrna Loy, and Rudolph Valentino.

In spite of the initial sensation it caused, the Columbia Gorge Hotel was a financial failure. Ironically, Simon Benson's beautiful, modern high-way caused the resort's downfall. Visitors from Portland could drive to Hood River in just three hours, enjoy the scenery and a sumptuous meal, then drive home. There was no need to spend the night — much less the summer — in the large, expensive hotel. After a year, a frustrated Benson sold the hotel to his son, Amos, who had no better luck. Even Thiele abandoned the hotel. In 1925, there was a foreclosure on the property.

For two decades the hotel struggled along, passed from owner to owner, many of them local people who poured money into it, hoping to recreate its glory days. The hotel finally closed during World War II. It reopened in 1952, not as a resort, but as a retirement home.

Later, a Portland businessman bought the building in hope of recreat-ing the Jazz Age resort. Investing $1 million in the renovation, he opened the hotel in 1979, but still could not make a profit. In 1982, the Columbia Gorge Hotel was sold at a sheriff's auction, then sold again within a month.

It ended up in the hands of Boyd Graves, a Seattle man whose family had owned the Snoqualmie Falls Lodge. Graves completed the renovation, succeeding at restoring much of the hotel's original look and original role in the Pacific Northwest: a romantic getaway known for its beauty, its luxury, and its fabulous food.

The Columbia Gorge Hotel today

Entering the Columbia Gorge Hotel, you notice a change of atmosphere, an air of femininity and formality. Everything is in deep shades of green and pink, all brass lamps and gold-framed mirrors. In the quiet lobby, a sculptured carpet budding with roses surrounds a circular velvet-covered settee, in the center an enormous bouquet of fresh-cut flowers. Upstairs, the attractive guest rooms are individually decorated, some with fine antiques like polished brass or canopy beds. One room is graced by a 200-year-old hand-carved bed, discovered in a castle in France.

In spite of the tasteful furnishings, much of the hotel's beauty is found outdoors. Its gardens, meticulously tended, bloom like an oasis alongside the Gorge. You can blissfully lose track of an entire afternoon here, admiring the views of river and waterfall, taking in the sunshine, stopping to sit in a hanging wooden swing, an island in an ocean of roses.

As in Henri Thiele's time, the hotel is perhaps best known as a restaurant. One magazine poll bestowed the Columbia River Court Dining Room with awards for the Best View, Best Service, and Best Breakfast, and for being the overall Best Restaurant. Dinners ($15-30) feature not only traditional local entrees like fillet mignon and Pacific salmon, but also unusual concoctions such as wilted spinach salad flambé for two. Don't miss breakfast. Complimentary for hotel guests (non-guests pay $23) and served all week long, the four-course "World Famous Farm Breakfast" will overwhelm you with everything from apple fritters to grilled mountain trout.

What to do along the Columbia Gorge

The Columbia Gorge is a favorite spot for **wind-surfing**; also popular are **bicycling, white-water rafting**, and **fishing**. The nearby town of **Hood River** has plenty of shops and restaurants, as well its own **historical museum**. Much of the gorge's beauty can seen by driving along sections of the original **Scenic Columbia River Highway**, which runs parallel to

Interstate 84 to the east and west of the hotel. Halfway between Portland and Hood River, stop for lunch at the 1925 **Multnomah Falls Lodge**. The **Bonneville Dam**, completed in 1939, is open for tours, as are several local **wineries**. An hour east of the hotel, just across the Columbia River, you can visit the **Maryhill Museum of Art**, a 1926 mansion which houses an extensive Rodin collection and, nearby, a full-sized replica of Stonehenge.

CHRISTINE UMMEL

The hotel's plush lobby revolves around a circular velvet-covered settee, topped with a bouquet of fresh-cut flowers.

Room Rates: $150 and up.

Restrictions: Smoking allowed in guest rooms but not in dining room.

Reservations: Four or five weeks in advance during the summer. For the rest of the year, a few days in advance is often enough.

Room Features: Private bathrooms, television sets, telephones.

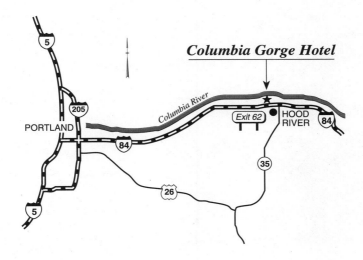

How to get there
From Interstate 5 near Portland, take Interstate 84 east along the Columbia River. After driving for about one hour, take Exit 62, west of Hood River, and make an immediate left. Cross the freeway, then take a left onto Westcliff. The hotel will be on your right.

The old brick Shaniko Hotel has survived decades of ups and downs as part of a Central Oregon ghost town.

Shaniko Hotel

P.O. Box 86
Shaniko, OR 97057
(503) 489-3441

History

If you want to get away from it all, Shaniko is the place for you. Set in the middle of the Central Oregon desert, this tiny ghost town has only thirty permanent residents. Walking down the dusty streets, past wooden buildings cracked and blackened by the passage of time, you find it hard to believe that Shaniko was once a center of trade, where millions of dollars exchanged hands. The secret of Shaniko's great prosperity — and its sudden demise — was the railroads.

Here's why: In the last half of the 1800s, ranchers used the hundreds of miles of open territory in Eastern Oregon as grazing land for cows and sheep. But the sheepherders had a problem: There was no easy way to transport their wool north to load onto the railroad that ran alongside the Columbia River. Then a group of bankers decided to build a branch of the railroad stretching from the Columbia south into Central Oregon. The tail end of the new Columbia Southern Railroad would be near the stagecoach station that a German immigrant named August Scherneckau had built in the 1870s. The local Indians, finding Scherneckau's foreign name too hard to pronounce, had called him "Shaniko," and the new town at the end of the railroad was christened "Shaniko" as well.

When the first train pulled into Shaniko in March 1900, it was greeted by a tent city of 100 men who were building the new town. That first train brought handmade bricks and freshly cut lumber for what would become one of the town's longest-lasting institutions: the Columbia Southern Hotel. Opened in 1902, the two-story red brick hotel was a place of luxury, with heat in every room and a balcony over the front porch, supported by stylish white columns. Surrounding it were all the necessary elements of a prosperous western town: a row of stores, a city hall, a schoolhouse, a water tower, a firehouse. Shaniko also had thirteen saloons and a sizable red light district.

For ten years Shaniko prospered. Sheepherders came from as far away as Idaho and California, driving wagons piled high with wool to be sold to merchants and loaded onto trains. The town's usual population of 600 would climb as high as 1,500 as dozens of wagon trains arrived for wool auctions held twice a year. In 1903, about $3 million in wool exchanged hands there. In 1904, the trade grew to $5 million. Shaniko was called "The Wool Capitol of the World."

Then, suddenly, Shaniko died. The year 1911 dealt the town two mortal blows. First, a rival railroad was built along the Deschutes River into Bend. Sheepherders no longer needed to bring their wool all the way north to Shaniko; Bend, farther south, was more convenient. Later in the year, a fire raged through town. The sturdy Columbia Southern Hotel, its brick walls eighteen inches thick, was unharmed, but most of the town's business district was destroyed. No one ever bothered to rebuild it.

From that year on, Shaniko's population dwindled. The Columbia Southern Hotel — which came to be called the Shaniko Hotel — survived, although it changed hands often. In 1921, the hotel was bought by Johnny McLennan, a Scottish immigrant who had made his money running sheep. McLennan owned the hotel for twenty-five years, and moved in himself when he retired from raising sheep. One afternoon, two strangers came to the hotel and registered for the night. By the next morning, they had disappeared, and so had McLennan. Days passed without a word from him. Three weeks later, he reappeared, distraught, and revealed that he had been abducted and forced to write checks. McLennan never recovered from his frightening experience, and died a year later.

Johnny McLennan's brother Duncan took over the hotel and ran it for twelve years, until he sold it to Joe and Sue Morelli in 1954. After Joe's death in 1971, Sue made ends meet by bringing in a group of mentally disabled elderly men, who boarded there under the state foster-care program. The "Shaniko Gang" helped run the hotel and the town, often playing the roles of "the cop" or "the sheriff" to the delight of visiting tourists. This lasted until 1977, when county officials ordered Morelli to improve the hotel's water and sewage facilities. Unable to afford the upgrade, Morelli auctioned off the property. The Shaniko Hotel was abandoned.

When Jean and Dorothy Farrell bought the hotel in 1985, it was a mess. Windows were smashed, the ceilings were full of holes, and the roof leaked. Over two and a half years, Jean Farrell spent about $500,000 on restoration — and that doesn't count any labor, which was all done by Farrell and volunteering friends. They completely gutted the second floor, reducing the number of rooms from twenty-eight to seventeen, and rebuilt the rotted-out front porch.

The Shaniko Hotel today

The Shaniko Hotel has a warm, simple, slightly rustic feel. Most of the lobby is original: the curved wooden staircase, the old front desk, the round settee wrapped around the pillar that holds up the ceiling. Other antiques — a player piano, a telephone switchboard, a wooden beer keg, an elk's head on the wall — contribute to the Wild West mood. Rocking chairs and love seats make this a cozy place to pass the time. In good weather, take a moment to relax on the hanging swing out on the front porch.

Rooms in the Shaniko Hotel are comfortable and clean, if plain. There's a wooden bed, a wooden chair, and a wooden night stand made to look like an old-fashioned ice box. The whole upstairs is decorated in contemporary shades of creme, gray, and rose, with long lace curtains over the windows. The fanciest room is the Bridal Suite, which has a Jacuzzi bath and a sitting area.

Room rates include breakfast in the morning, a big plus. The dining room off the lobby serves up meals designed to fill up hungry ranchers — French toast, eggs, stacks of thick pancakes. For lunch and dinner, there's hearty, old-fashioned fare such as meatloaf and chicken-fried steak. After dinner, stop in the hotel's gift shop for a peek at the old steel safe behind the counter; this room once housed the town's bank.

What to do in Shaniko

There's not enough in Shaniko to occupy you for very long, but you can spend an entertaining afternoon there exploring. **Antique shops** occupy the rickety buildings across the street, along with a tiny turquoise **wedding chapel**. A barn down the road houses a rusty collection of **antique cars** from the 1920s and 1930s. Kids may enjoy taking a **stage coach ride** or throwing back a sarsaparilla in the **Stagecoach Saloon.** All the buildings in town are original, except for the post office, which is a reproduction. Look for the **water tower**, the **schoolhouse**, the **city hall** and **town jail**, and the **blacksmith's shop**. (Warning: except for the hotel, most of Shaniko is only open during the summer, because the old buildings have no heating systems.) Nearby attractions include the **John Day Fossil Beds**, about twenty miles to the east, and **fishing** and **white-water rafting** on the Deschutes River.

Room Rates: $55 for a double, $85 for the Bridal Suite.

Restrictions: No smoking in rooms, no pets.

Reservations: Recommended on weekdays, necessary on weekends.

Room Features: Private baths, no telephones or television sets.

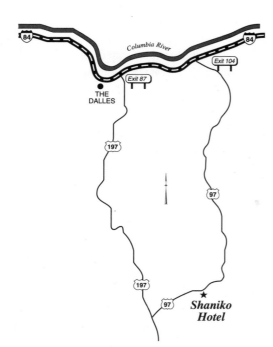

How to get there

From Interstate 5, get on Interstate 84 east near Portland. Follow the Columbia River until you reach The Dalles. Then drive south on Highway 197 for about one hour. Turn left onto Highway 97 headed north. Take a right turn into Shaniko; the hotel will be on your left.

Timberline Lodge

Timberline Ski Area
Timberline Lodge, OR 97028
(503) 231-5400 / (800) 547-1406

History

The year was 1936.

One of four U.S. workers was unemployed. President Franklin D. Roosevelt's Works Progress Administration (WPA) was organizing make-work projects to put millions of impoverished Americans back to work. One of the most impressive projects was the Timberline Lodge.

Four stories high and over 400 feet long, the lodge on Mt. Hood was built entirely by hand — no electric tools were used. The first story was made of concrete and native boulders to create a base that would blend into the side of the mountain. For the upper stories, huge timbers cut with broad axes were shaped into beams and columns. Steeply pitched roofs, covered in cedar shingles, were erected to allow heavy snowpacks to slide off. At the center of the Alpine-style lodge was a hexagonal-shaped "Head House," built around a gigantic ninety-two-foot-high stone fireplace.

Life wasn't easy for the WPA workers constructing the massive lodge. Far from their families, these older men (their average age was fifty-five) worked long hours, often in near-freezing temperatures. Crews of as many as 150 men worked at a time, and were switched every two weeks in order to employ as many people as possible. They earned ninety cents an hour, plus room (eight men to a tent) and board (three hot meals a day).

Still, many of them came to love their work. Master craftsmen taught them stonemasonry, carpentry, and blacksmithing. Previously unskilled

117

During the Depression, hundreds of laborers and craftsmen were put to work building the Timberline Lodge on Mt. Hood.

hands learned to forge iron into door hinges, light fixtures, furniture, and ornamental gates. Other men became wood carvers, creating tables and chairs, bears and buffalo heads. When the lodge was completed in 1938, many of these strong, proud men left with tears in their eyes, saying it had been the most interesting work of their lives.

Men weren't solely responsible for the lodge, however. An army of women was hired to help furnish the lodge. They wove fabric, upholstered chairs and couches, hooked rugs, and appliquéed colorful patterns onto curtains and bedspreads, all by hand. The project also supported local artists, who were commissioned to create paintings, relief carvings, and mosaics for the lodge.

Hard as it is to believe considering the high cost of the lodge (over $1 million), many of the materials had been recycled. The tops of telephone poles were carved into eagles, coyotes, and other woodland creatures to become posts on the front stairway. Worn-out blankets and uniforms were

118

cut into strips and hand-hooked into rugs. Fireplace andirons were made from old railroad tracks.

On September 28, 1937, President Roosevelt came to Mt. Hood by motorcade to dedicate the Timberline Lodge. In his speech, delivered from the great stone balcony and broadcast on national radio, Roosevelt described the lodge as "a monument to the skill and faithful performance of workers on the rolls of the Works Progress Administration."

Yet almost from its grand opening in 1938, the lodge suffered from financial problems. Skiing there had not yet caught on, and various managers found it nearly impossible to attract enough guests to the fifty-room lodge to pay for its enormous upkeep costs. In February of 1955, the lodge was closed. The electrical company had turned off its power because of unpaid bills. Many residents of Portland, fifty-five miles away, discussed closing the Timberline permanently.

Then a twenty-nine-year-old social worker, Richard Kohnstamm, came forward. Determined to save the lodge, Kohnstamm borrowed money from his brother and sister to form the R. L. K. Company, which took over management of the lodge and remodeled it. Even then the lodge had some economic close calls until skiing became popular there in the early 1960s. Now managed by Kohnstamm's son Jeff, the Timberline Lodge is today one of the best-known ski resorts in America, attracting Olympic ski teams from all over the world and more than 1.5 million visitors every year.

That popularity has had its drawbacks. Over the years, many of the lodge's original furnishings — especially fragile items such as curtains and upholstery — have become damaged or worn out. Since 1975, an organization called the Friends of Timberline has worked to restore the lodge's arts and crafts treasures. Under their sponsorship, local artists and craftspeople have carved furniture, sewn curtains, hooked rugs, and performed a variety of other tasks using the original blueprints and the same natural materials and pioneer techniques as the lodge's creators in the 1930s. Their work has helped make the Timberline Lodge the living museum it is today.

The Timberline Lodge today

Rooms at the lodge are big and comfortable, rustically decorated in simple designs and bold colors. All the wood and metalwork creates a warm, pioneer-like atmosphere. It's hard to believe that it's all handmade, from the patterned bedspreads to the parchment lampshades on the twisted iron reading lamps. A few contemporary touches — television sets and modern bathrooms are the main examples — don't spoil the effect. The decor is especially colorful in the eight "fireplace rooms," which are large enough to be considered suites and all have their own fireplaces.

Geographically and socially the center of the lodge, the rough-hewn Head House serves as a living room for skiers, climbers, and tourists. It's also an impressive showplace for the lodge's artwork and mementos. On the top floor, drinks are served in the Rams Head Bar. The modest-looking Cascade Dining Room is well known for its incredible Northwest cuisine. Unusual dinners such as salmon ravioli cost $15-30. Soups and sandwiches can be enjoyed in the cheerful Blue Ox Deli downstairs. While you're exploring the Head House, keep a lookout for Heidi, the most recent in a series of friendly Saint Bernards to watch over the Timberline Lodge.

What to do on Mt. Hood

In the lodge, you'll find a **heated pool**, a **sauna**, and a **Jacuzzi**. Be sure to visit the **exhibition center** in the lower lobby to learn more about the history of Timberline Lodge. Probably the most popular activity on the mountain is **skiing**, which lasts from November until Labor Day. This is also one of the most popular mountains in the world for **snowboarding** and **mountain-climbing**. Beginning climbers can hire mountain guides to take them on day trips. **Hiking trails** are used by the public except in winter. Stop for lunch and a tour of the **Mt. Hood Brewing Co. and Brew Pub** at Government Camp. Nearby, on the **Mt. Hood Railroad**, Pullman coaches from the early 1900s take visitors on a scenic ride through the Hood River Valley.

Room Rates: Rooms $60-140, fireplace rooms $160.

Reservations: Several months in advance for weekends.

Restrictions: No pets. Skis must be checked into lockers.

Room Features: Television sets, telephones. Most rooms with private bathrooms.

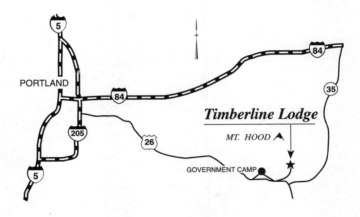

How to get there

From Interstate 5, take Interstate 84 east from Portland. Then head south on Interstate 205 until you can switch onto Highway 26. Continue on this road east all the way to Mount Hood, then follow signs to Government Camp and the Timberline Lodge.

CHRISTINE UMMEL

On a bluff forty feet above the sand and surf, this three-story clapboard hotel spent decades as a favorite honeymoon spot.

Sylvia Beach Hotel

267 NW Cliff Street
Newport, OR 97365
(503) 265-5428

History

You will not find the Sylvia Beach Hotel on Sylvia Beach. No such place exists, at least not in the oceanside resort town of Newport, Oregon.

The Sylvia Beach Hotel got its name from one of four enterprising women who dominate its history: the wife of a chicken rancher, two best friends from Portland, and an American lady in Paris who opened a very special bookstore.

The hotel is located on a forty-foot bluff overlooking Nye Beach. First occupied by a small boarding house, the property was purchased by a man named W. D. Wheeler in 1912. He tore down the Cliff House and built the New Cliff House, a large, three-story clapboard hotel covered in green shingles. Wheeler ran the hotel for nine years, then, tired of managing it, swapped careers with his friend Peter Gilmore. The Gilmores were given the hotel, and Wheeler took over their chicken ranch just outside of town.

Eight years after the trade, Peter Gilmore died in an automobile accident. His wife, Cecile, became the new proprietor and ran the hotel successfully for the next thirty years. The Hotel Gilmore, as it was called then, wasn't fancy, but its beach-side location and moderate prices drew tourists from all over Oregon. Until highways were constructed in the late 1930s, people had to take the train to Toledo, then ride a ferry for the last ten miles along the coast. Under Cecile Gilmore's care, the Hotel Gilmore became a favorite destination for newlyweds, and was known as the Honeymoon Capital of the Oregon Coast.

After Cecile Gilmore sold it in 1957, the hotel went through a series of owners, but maintained its basic character. The change came in the early 1960s, when the Gilmore was first used as a residential hotel. Over the next twenty-five years, not much money was spent on the hotel's maintenance and the Gilmore gradually deteriorated — as did its clientele. By the mid-1980s, the hotel had become a flophouse, home to a handful of starving poets and unpublished authors, as well as drug addicts and derelicts.

That was the condition in which Gudrun "Goody" Cable found it. The owner of a Portland coffeehouse, Cable had been looking for an old hotel to turn into a gathering place for book lovers. She knew the Gilmore was the perfect location, but didn't think she could fulfill the dream by herself. So Cable recruited the help of Sally Ford, who had been her best friend since grade school. Together they purchased the old hotel, and borrowed enough money to renovate it. Many of the old tenants were unhappy about leaving — it wasn't everywhere you could get a room with an ocean view for $50 a month.

The inspiration for the hotel's new look would be a woman named Sylvia Beach. In 1919, this American lady opened a bookstore in Paris that carried only books in English. The Shakespeare & Company Bookstore became a gathering place for American expatriate writers, the hangout of Ernest Hemmingway, Scott Fitzgerald, Ezra Pound, Gertrude Stein, and D. H. Lawrence. Sylvia Beach was a patron of the arts, encouraging people to read, to write, and to publish their work. When no publisher would touch James Joyce's racey novel *Ulysseus*, Sylvia Beach published it herself.

To create a literary hotel worthy of bearing Sylvia Beach's name, Ford and Cable recruited the help of twenty friends. After remodeling the interior to create twenty rooms with private bathrooms, they assigned each friend a room to decorate in honor of a favorite author. The chosen writers ranged from Somerset Maughm to Dr. Seuss. After one and a half years of work, the hotel was ready for its grand opening on March 14, 1987, Sylvia Beach's centennial birthday.

The Sylvia Beach Hotel today

Every room in the Sylvia Beach Hotel is unique. The Agatha Christie Room, for instance, is decidedly British, furnished in dark greens and wooden antiques. Mystery fans will recognize clues from Christie's novels hidden around the room: bullet casings in the wall, men's shoes sticking out from behind the draperies, a tiny clay figurine of an elephant. The Tennessee Williams Room (called "Stella!") has white wicker furniture and a mosquito veil over the bed — true Southern style. In the Herman Melville Room, you'll find framed prints of whaling schooners, an old sailor's chest, and a mirror shaped like a porthole. The Alice Walker Room has a strong African flavor, while the Meride Le Sueur room bears Native American accents. You may find it difficult to sleep in the Edgar Allen Poe Room; a stuffed raven watches over this realm of nightmare-black and blood-red, where a sharpened pendulum hangs over the bed.

Each room comes with a collection of books written by its namesake author. There's also a journal to record your thoughts; some of the remarks recorded in these journals have developed into extended conversations between people who have never met.

Every book lover will enjoy the informal double-decker library upstairs. There you can browse through a collection of books, play with board games and jigsaw puzzles, or just lay back in a deep armchair and enjoy the spectacular ocean view. On the ground floor, the gift shop/bookstore offers a wide variety of titles and literary paraphernalia. Take a minute to examine the mural on the lobby wall: It shows Sylvia Beach and James Joyce seated together in the Shakespeare & Company Bookstore. Whenever published authors visit the hotel, they're asked to sign their names on the books on the shelves in the mural. Downstairs, in the "Table of Contents," guests meet over eight-person tables for elaborate seafood dinners (about $17), a total of eight "chapters" from appetizer to dessert.

What to do in Newport

For over 100 years, most of Newport's visitors have come for one thing — the spectacular **beaches**. Most of the entertainment here is somehow related to the ocean; there's **boating**, **wind-surfing**, **deep-sea fishing**, **whale-watching**, **crabbing**, and **scuba-diving**. The town boasts several aquariums, including the **Oregon Coast Aquarium**, Oregon State University's **Marine Science Center**, and the **Undersea Gardens**. To experience a taste of Newport's past, visit the town's oldest building, the 1871 **Yaquina Bay Lighthouse**. The **Burrows House**, built in 1895, holds a museum about the region's Victorian period, while the **Log Cabin Museum** explores the town's Native American and pioneer heritage.

Room Rates: Rooms $60-90, suites $130.

Restrictions: No smoking whatsoever.

Reservations: Must be made two to three months in advance for summer days, holidays, or weekends.

Room Features: Private bathrooms, no telephones, no television sets.

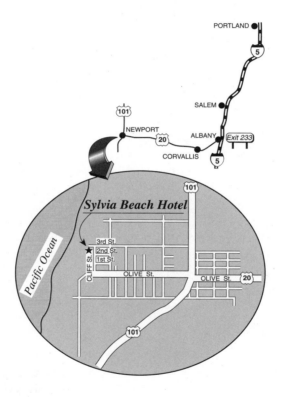

How to get there
From Interstate 5, take Exit 233 at Albany onto Highway 20 and head west. After about one hour, you'll reach Newport and the highway will become Olive Street. Turn right onto Cliff Street and drive north for three blocks. The hotel will be on your left, at the corner of NW Third Street and Cliff Street.

Wolf Creek Tavern

P.O. Box 97
Wolf Creek, OR 97497
(503) 866-2474

History

"With a final spurt, the dusty six-horse stage team dashed up to a welcome light that beamed through the early dusk. 'Wolf Creek!' sang out the driver as he clamped on the brakes."

When this narrative was written for a publicity brochure in the 1920s, the Wolf Creek Tavern was already a historic landmark. The inn is so old that nobody knows exactly how old it is. Some stories claim it was built in 1857 by railroad tycoon Ben Holladay or by Chinese immigrants mining for gold. Most historical research, however, indicates that local entrepreneur Henry Smith built the tavern sometime between 1868 and 1873.

At that time, a 710-mile wagon road (roughly parallel to today's Interstate 5) stretched from Portland to Sacramento. For fifty dollars, you could make the trip by stage coach in six days. About every ten miles along this route was a stagecoach station, where worn-out horses could be changed and weary passengers could eat or spend the night.

Stage coaches didn't stop regularly at Wolf Creek. The nearest station was in Grave Creek, but genteel travelers were willing to ride a few more miles by horse to stay at the Wolf Creek Tavern. This Classical Revival inn, with its white pillars and two-story veranda, had ten guest rooms, a dining room, a ballroom, a ladies' parlor, and a men's sitting room. Heavy drinking had to be done elsewhere, however. Smith was a strict teetotaler and would allow no alcohol in his "tavern" (then the term meant an inn or

Genteel travelers, riding the stage coach from Sacramento to Portland, would stop for the night at the Wolf Creek Tavern.

boarding house, not a saloon). Many of Smith's guests allegedly visited another establishment nearby, called the "Gallon House" because it sold whiskey in that quantity.

The tavern proved highly profitable for Smith, as were his sawmills and gold-mining operations. Though wealthy, he distrusted banks and insisted on burying his money. According to local legend, when Smith fell ill and figured he was on his deathbed, he sent for his best friend, presumably to tell him the location of his fortune. By the time the friend arrived at the hospital, it was too late. Smith was dead, and his money never was found. Residents of Wolf Creek still look occasionally for Smith's buried treasure.

After Smith's death, the tavern was operated by a series of private owners. The stage coaches that had brought its visitors were replaced first by railroads, then by freeways. John "Bud" Dougall and his wife "Dinky" purchased the inn in 1922 and had good luck with it, especially because the new Pacific Highway brought a steady stream of tourists to their door. In 1927, the Dougalls constructed a new south wing, which added new guest rooms to the tavern, as well as its first indoor bathroom.

Throughout its lifetime, the Wolf Creek Tavern was often a favorite retreat of the rich and famous. Movie stars Mary Pickford and Clark Gable stayed here. So did authors Zane Grey and Sinclair Lewis. After his visit, legendary motion-picture director Orson Welles left the proprietors a note reading: "To be or not to be; That was some chicken!" Jack London stayed in the tavern in 1911 with his wife Charmain. While he hunted and fished, she finished typing his story "The End of the Story."

The tavern became a rowdier place during the 1950s, when local timber workers used it as a bar and clubhouse. They would come here for a beer after work, the metal spikes on the loggers' boots chewing up the wood floors. In the 1960s, the building was used as a commune by a group of flower children, who ate vegetarian food and reportedly grew marijuana in one of the bathtubs.

After 100 years of almost continual use, the Wolf Creek Tavern began to show its age in the 1970s. The Oregon State Parks and Recreation Department bought the property in 1975 and began a meticulous restoration of the inn. Wainscoting, doors, and moldings had to be hand-finished. Original paint colors were reproduced for the walls, wood work, and chimneys. Eight guest rooms were each given a private bath and antique furniture reflecting the inn's stagecoach days. Though the building still belongs to the State Parks, the Wolf Creek Tavern is once again run by private hoteliers, a wayside inn for the weary traveler.

The Wolf Creek Tavern today

The Wolf Creek Tavern has a quiet authenticity that makes it a rare find. The main "L" of the inn is decorated with antiques from the 1880s, like rocking chairs and hurricane lamps, while the south wing has furniture from the 1920s, when it was constructed. With wood plank floors and patchwork quilts, the rooms are rustic and simple — not frilly, because a stagecoach stop was never fancy.

In fact, the sitting room downstairs (once the ladies' parlor) may be too elegant to honestly recapture the tavern's past. Velvet Victorian armchairs surround a square grand piano, older than tavern itself. A gold-trimmed clock sits on the mantle of the brick fireplace, its pendulum hypnotically ticking away the slow hours.

Across the hall, the men's sitting room is now a bar, but you can still see boot marks on the fireplace where men warmed their feet by the fire. The dining room next door, run by waitresses in turn-of-the-century garb, offers sautéed scallops, chicken almondine, and other dishes for $10-15. In spite of their aristocratic names, meals are cooked country style with generous portions of rice, potatoes and vegetables.

What to do in Wolf Creek

The town of Wolf Creek is tiny — just a post office, general store, gas station and cafe — but it's surrounded by the great outdoors. **Hiking trails and country roads** wind through the nearby mountains, including one to "London Peak," named for the famous author. **Fishing** and **river-rafting** are popular on the Rogue River. The ghost town of **Golden**, only four miles away, was a prosperous gold-mining community in the 1800s, and was once used as a setting for "Gunsmoke." The nearest city is **Grants Pass.**

Room Rates: $55 per night for one or two people, $75 for the master suite.

Reservations: Advised but not always necessary. Call two to three weeks in advance.

Restrictions: Smoking okay, children okay.

Room Features: Private bathrooms. Television sets and telephones are available upon request.

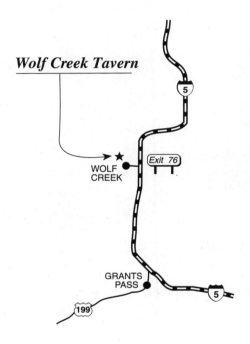

How to get there
From Interstate 5, take Exit 76, twenty miles north of Grants Pass. Take the main road north a little way; the tavern will be on your left.

Covered in rough cedar bark, this mountain lodge resembles a great tree rising out of the forests of the Siskiyou Mountains.

Oregon Caves Chateau

P.O. Box 128
Cave Junction, OR 97523
(503) 592-3400

History

Elijah Davidson ran through the forest, calling for his dog.

Twenty-five-year-old Davidson and his dog Bruno had been hunting in the Siskiyou Mountains near their home when Bruno suddenly caught the scent of a bear and charged after it. The enthusiastic dog followed the bear into a hole in the side of the mountain. Hearing a fight break out between the two animals, Davidson tightened his grip on his rifle and rushed into the opening. Inside it was dark and cold. Striking a match, Davidson found himself lost in an alien world of marble caverns and underground streams, a strange place nature had sculpted secretly over thousands of years, where stone flowed in waves, ripples, and waterfalls, and dripped from the ceilings like icicles.

Davidson and Bruno made it out of the caves; they even bagged the bear. Back at home, Davidson described the beautiful caves he had discovered that November day in 1874. Soon, adventurers were coming from miles around to explore the mysterious passageways. One party unrolled a ball of string as they went along, to keep them from getting lost in the labyrinth. Whoever was holding the string accidentally dropped it, though, and it took the explorers two hours to find their way out.

Though fond of the caves, visitors weren't always kind to them. Many people carved their names in the walls or broke off stone formations to take home as souvenirs. Local entrepreneurs, trying to develop a tourist attraction, often were reckless in their "improvement" of the caves. One expedition in 1894 invaded with drills, hammers, and dynamite, blasting their way into new cave rooms.

In 1907, the caves had a special visitor: Joaquin Miller, considered the poet laureate of the West. Miller's praise of "Oregon's Marble Halls" in *Sunset* magazine brought the caves national publicity. Concerned about vandalism, Miller teamed up with local conservationists and politicians to lobby for protection of the caves, their cause reaching all the way to Washington, D.C. On July 12, 1909, President William Howard Taft declared the Oregon Caves a national monument.

After that, the caves' popularity skyrocketed. More cautious improvements were made: rooms were opened up, steel ladders and walkways put in, electric lighting installed. In 1922, when a new road to the caves was completed, fifteen hundred visitors arrived to celebrate "Cave Day."

However, all the visitors — 10,000 of them in 1922 — had to sleep in tent houses. A small chalet was built in 1922, but the number of guests soon outgrew it. In 1929 the resort's manager unveiled plans to build a six-story $50,000 chateau. The designer would be Gust Lium, a maverick local architect who sketched his plans on napkins and scraps of paper.

Like many old buildings, the Oregon Caves Chateau has its resident ghost, Elizabeth. In life, Elizabeth was staying at the lodge with her husband when she found out that he was having an affair with one of the cleaning ladies. Distraught, she hung herself in the closet. (That's the story, anyway. The lodge's files have no record of a suicide.) Although rumored to hold a grudge against all cleaning ladies, Elizabeth never does any harm. She just moves objects around and occasionally plays the lobby piano.

Elizabeth's tragic story notwithstanding, the Oregon Caves Chateau is apparently a good place for romance. Many employees met their spouses here, or are the children of couples who met while working here. According to one of the most incredible stories, a woman visiting the caves during the Depression heard the sound of a saxophone echoing through the hills at night. Later, she was in a Chicago coffee shop and took the only seat available. Talking to the man next to her, she mentioned the Oregon Caves and the music. She discovered that her new friend had been an employee at the caves — and had loved practicing the saxophone at night! The two of them were later married.

Lium's design was certainly unique. Though patterned after a Swiss chalet, the outside of the lodge was covered in rough cedar bark, so it looked like a huge tree growing out of the ravine. Most of the lodge was made of native materials. Douglas fir was used for the support beams in the dining room and lobby. The main staircase was built of oak, madrona, and fir, the roof covered in redwood shingles. The big double fireplace in the lobby was made of the marble, blasted out of the hillside to make room for the lodge. Part of Cave Creek was diverted to flow through the middle of the dining room.

Although the Chateau itself was completed in 1934, the land around it was not landscaped until years later. During the Great Depression, the Civilian Conservation Corps built retaining walls, a campfire circle, trout pools, and waterfalls.

Since then, the Oregon Caves and the Chateau have had their ups and downs, including a flood that poured down the mountain in 1964, filling the Chateau's bottom floor with mud. Over the past fifty years, most work at the Oregon Caves has been done to maintain what's there — or to repair damage done by the caves' early explorers. Now a national historic landmark, the Chateau looks much as it did in 1934 and it serves the same purpose: to be a comfortable resting place for visitors to this natural wonder.

The Oregon Caves Chateau today

Rooms at the Chateau are large and comfortable, though a bit campy with their loud orange carpets and mustard-brown walls. Most charming is the third floor. There each room is a different shape, some with triangular, vaulted ceilings. They're furnished with the original 1934 beds, dressers, and chairs, hand-painted with horses or bouquets of flowers.

Downstairs, the lobby is a classic. The wooden armchairs and the rawhide leather lampshades date back to the Chateau's opening. Displayed there are a valuable collection of Kaiser photographs (black-and-white photos hand-tinted with oil paints) and a grandfathers clock over 100 years old. Dinner is served throughout the summer in the formal dining room on the first floor. For breakfast or lunch, visit the 1930s-style coffee shop.

What to do at the Oregon Caves

The Oregon Caves Company gives **tours of the caves** several times a day. Tour rates are $6.75 for adults, $3.75 for children aged six to eleven. The caves are cold and slippery, so bring a warm sweater and good boots or shoes. Outside the caves are a number of **hiking trails** through Siskiyou National Forest. The park service also provides **interpretive services** and **campfire programs** during the summer.

CHRISTINE UMMEL

Visitors have been exploring these strange, beautiful marble caves for more than 100 years.

Room Rates: One or two people $79, three people $88, four people $97.

Reservations: Recommended thirty days in advance.

Restrictions: No pets.

Room Features: Private bathrooms, no television sets or telephones.

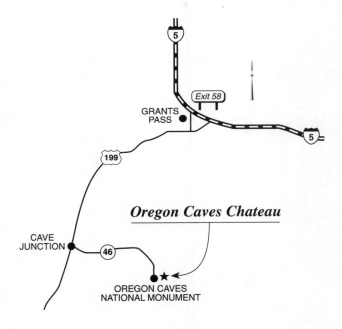

How to get there
From Interstate 5, take Exit 58 in Grants Pass. Get on Highway 199 and drive south for about one hour until you reach Cave Junction. Then take Highway 46 into the mountains to the Oregon Caves National Monument.

CHRISTINE UMMEL

In 1860, this sturdy brick building was constructed as part of a booming gold rush town. Only recently has it become a popular hotel.

Jacksonville Inn

175 E California Street
Jacksonville, OR 97530
1-800-321-9344

History

"Gold!"

The cry that triggered stampedes to California in 1849 had the same effect on Southern Oregon just two years later. In 1851, James Cluggage and John Poole were traveling south, bringing supplies from the north to sell to gold-diggers in California, when they stopped for the night alongside Daisy Creek in the foothills of Oregon's Siskiyou Mountains. As the legend goes, the next morning the men were packing up their mules when they noticed a gold nugget sticking out of a muddy hoofprint.

Cluggage and Poole hurried to stake their claims to the area. Their precious secret, however, soon leaked out. Within months, the two prospectors had more than one thousand new neighbors. The large number of gold prospectors attracted farmers, shopkeepers, bankers, and saloon keepers. A tent city sprang up, soon replaced by wooden buildings, then brick ones. First called "Rich Gulch" or "Table Rock City," this boom town later was named "Jacksonville."

One early settler was Patrick J. Ryan, a successful merchant responsible for many of Jacksonville's stores and houses. In 1860, Ryan bought a plot of land on Jacksonville's main street and built a one-story brick storehouse. The bricks came from one of the town's earliest industries, the Jacksonville Kiln. Walls of the basement were made of sandstone from local quarries, and it's said you can see specks of gold dust in the mortar.

139

Ryan was especially proud that his building, built of solid brick, was fireproof. Then, in 1873, a fire broke out. The *Oregon Sentinel* reported that "From the United States Hotel the fire spread with almost lightning speed and soon the whole block was in flames ... including the supposed fireproof [building] of Mr. P. J. Ryan." Sustaining $30,000 in damages, Ryan was one of the heaviest losers in town.

The following year, Ryan not only repaired the building, but added a brick second floor as well. Then he built a third-story "penthouse" out of wood. The third floor was removed around the turn of the century, but for a time Ryan's building was the tallest that Jacksonville had ever seen.

Besides changing in appearance, Ryan's building underwent frequent changes in use. At first Ryan rented out its rooms to Henry Judge, a harness and saddle maker, and H. Bloom, a Russian-born merchant. Later it became the home of Morris Mensor's General Merchandise. Ryan himself ran the store for a while, selling cloth, groceries, and hardware. During its long lifetime, the building also would be used as a clothing store, a livery stable, a laundry, and an apartment building. It's rumored that the building once was occupied by numerous ladies of the evening, whom town authorities eventually removed.

Jacksonville had fallen on hard times. First the area's gold deposits had started to run out. During the 1860s and 1870s, the town had been hit by a small pox epidemic, a devastating flood, and the terrible fire. Then, in 1884, the Oregon and California Railroad passed, not by Jacksonville, but five miles to the east. A new town, Medford, grew up around the terminal, but Jacksonville — once the largest town in all of Oregon — faded into obscurity.

Conditions in Jacksonville became so desperate during the Great Depression that townspeople started looking for gold again. Many dug enough gold out of their backyards to keep food on the dinner table. One mine shaft was dug in the basement of the P. J. Ryan Building, and tunneled under Jacksonville's main street. Later a large truck was driving through town when the street suddenly collapsed underneath it.

Things began to turn around for Jacksonville in the 1960s, as tourists discovered the quaint gold-mining community. In 1966, the entire town was declared a National Historic Landmark. Among those drawn to the area was Jack Bate, a local businessman who purchased the old P. J. Ryan Building in 1968.

To recreate it as the Jacksonville Inn, Bate gutted the inside of the building to construct guestrooms and a restaurant. Bates went to great lengths to use building materials from the historically correct era. The original bricks, though re-laid for eveness, were used in walls and floors. Supporting beams in the bar and foyer were taken from an early-day sawmill on the Umpqua River. Whip-sawed lumber, salvaged from a mid-nineteenth-century building, became the outdoor staircase. Now owned by Jerry and Linda Evans, the inn has eight guest rooms, each one named after an early settler, like P. J. Ryan, who helped build Jacksonville.

The Jacksonville Inn today

Don't let the plain brick facade fool you. Inside, the Jacksonville Inn is plushly decorated with both western antiques and modern luxuries. A few rooms may even be a little too flowery. Most romantic is Room 1, the honeymoon suite. As in all the rooms, rough brick walls remind you of the town's rugged past, but the rest is all elegance — swirling blue seashell wallpaper, antique furniture in dark wood, old-fashioned brass lamps, and long folded curtains. The four-poster bed is covered in white lace; sunk into one corner is a two-person Jacuzzi bathtub.

One drawback to the Jacksonville Inn is that there's no lobby or sitting room. However, you'll want to spend some time in the luxurious, ruby red dining room; it's one of the most highly acclaimed restaurants in Oregon. Gourmet dinners ($15-20) include veal scaloppini, prime rib, and chicken puff pastry, while the incredible breakfasts feature dishes such as omelets, smoked salmon, brioche French toast, and Belgium waffles. Light lunches and suppers can be enjoyed in the less-formal Bistro or on the pleasant backyard patio.

What to do around Jacksonville

You'll want to spend time simply strolling through town, admiring the **mid-nineteenth-century buildings**, which house shops, galleries, and fine restaurants. At the east end of town, there's the **Jacksonville Museum of Southern Oregon History**. Kids may prefer the **Children's Museum** next door. It's a ten-minute walk west up the hill to the **Jacksonville Cemetery**, where you'll find tombstones of early settlers and a good view of the valley. Every summer thousands come to Jacksonville for the **Britt Music Festival**, featuring performers from around the world. Modern entertain-

141

ment can be found in **Medford**, five miles to the east.

Room Rates: Rooms $80-95, honeymoon suite $125, separate honeymoon cottage $175. Full breakfast included with all rooms.

Reservations: Recommended one or two months in advance for the summer.

Restrictions: No smoking in rooms, no pets allowed.

Room Features: Private bathrooms, television sets, telephones, mini-refrigerators.

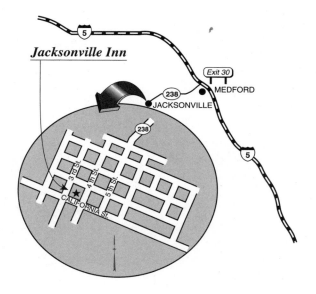

How to get there
From Interstate 5, take Exit 30 in Medford onto Highway 238. Go west for six miles until you reach Jacksonville, where the road becomes Fifth Street. Turn right onto California Street. The inn will be on your right, between Third Street and Fourth Street. Parking is in the back.

Mark Antony Hotel

212 E Main Street
Ashland, OR 97520
(503) 482-1721

History

The history of Ashland is the story of a town that tried for decades to become a tourist attraction, and finally succeeded. The history of the Mark Antony is the story of a hotel that's still trying.

Founded in 1852, Ashland was built around mining, farming, and logging. Its first taste of glory came in 1892. Ashland was chosen as a site for the Chautauqua, a traveling program of entertainers and lecturers meant to bring culture to the rural west. To accommodate its distinguished visitors, the town built the "Chautauqua tabernacle." In this beehive-shaped auditorium, families from all over applauded star performers such as opera singer Madame Schumann-Heink, actress Charlotte Greenwood, and John Phillip Sousa and his band.

When Chautauqua's popularity faded, townspeople looked for a new source of fame — in their water. All around town were natural mineral springs, especially springs of lithia water, which contained sodium, calcium, bicarbonate, and other "healthful minerals." The plan was to make Ashland a resort where tourists would come to bathe in and drink the health-giving waters. The town spent several years and hundreds of thousands of dollars to pipe the mineral water into town, and to landscape nineteen-acre Lithia Park, hoping to make Ashland "the playground of the Pacific Coast."

Over lunch one day in 1923, the Ashland Kiwanis Club decided the

Nine stories high, the Mark Antony towers over the rest of Ashland, a souvenir of the town's early attempts to become a health spa.

144

town needed a luxury hotel. To pay for it, the "Lithia Hotel Committee" sold stock in the project, raising $100,000 in just two days. With nine stories and ninety-nine rooms, the reinforced concrete hotel would, for many years, be the tallest building between Portland and San Francisco.

The new "Lithia Springs Hotel" was a wild mixture of architectural styles, a sample of the historic eclecticism that later would become Art Deco. Eagles peered down over the entrance; shields and ribbons sparkled in the stained-glass windows. The two-story lobby boasted a Venetian terrazzo floor, ornamental beams and pillars, and a mezzanine. The hotel had its own dining room, ballroom, barber shop, pharmacy, flower shop, candy store, and photographer. To tie in with the health resort plan, lithia spring water was piped directly into the hotel.

Opened in 1925, the hotel was a great success initially. However, Ashland never caught on as a health spa. In 1927, the Southern Pacific Railroad, which had brought visitors to Ashland, changed its route, skirting Southern Oregon on the way to Portland and Seattle. The Great Depression, coupled with competition from the modern new motels, almost killed the fancy Lithia Springs Hotel.

After some twenty-five years of financial floundering, the hotel was purchased by Jack Pumphrey, a Sacramento businessman. He tried to turn the hotel around by modernizing it. The dining room, with its high ceiling and Spanish plaster walls, was transformed into a modern bar and restaurant with red vinyl booths and synthetic paneling. Pumphrey also built a swimming pool and carpeted the lobby's patterned tile floor.

About that time, a third Ashland attraction began to get attention. In 1935, a young schoolteacher, inspired by the resemblance between the ruins of the Chautauqua tabernacle and sketches of Shakespeare's Globe Theater, started a festival of plays on the site. Ashland's "Oregon Shakespeare Festival" had acquired a national following by the 1960s. To cash in on the festival's growing popularity, Pumphrey renamed the hotel after Mark Antony, a key character in two of Shakespeare's plays. (It was a difficult adjustment: A helicopter, trying to remove the electric "Lithia Hotel" sign from the roof, almost crashed. It dropped the heavy sign, which caved in much of the hotel's ninth floor.)

Not even the Shakespeare Festival could bring the hotel success. It went through a succession of owners and transformations; one company brought in exotic dancers, who performed in the bar until city officials shut them down. The Mark Antony's most influential owner was Karsten Arriens, another Sacramento businessman. During the late 1970s, Arriens worked to restore the hotel's 1925 appearance. He spent over $900,000 on antique furnishings, renovated the lobby and dining room, and decorated the hallways with colorful, gold-trimmed murals. Arriens reopened the hotel and placed it on the National Historic Register, but still went bankrupt in 1982. The hotel's current owner, Joe Burkhardt, has been able to keep the hotel open, but not to complete the renovation begun by Arriens. For over five years, Burkhardt has been looking for someone to buy the hotel and invest enough money in it to realize its full potential.

The Mark Antony Hotel today

Stuck in the middle of a major renovation, the Mark Antony Hotel has a split personality. Guest rooms, especially, are a mixed bag. Some of the suites, particularly the eleven-hundred series (i.e., Room 811, Room 911, etc.) are gorgeous, furnished with exquisite antique bedroom sets. Some rooms have been redecorated recently, with new curtains and coats of paint. Other rooms are spartan, with barren white walls and scratched antiques.

To get to your room, you either have to climb several flights of stairs or wait for the hotel's single, painfully slow elevator. (The staff blames the elevator's uncooperative nature on spirits, disturbed because the hotel was built on an Indian burial ground. A more mundane explanation is that the 70-year-old elevator is simply slowing down in its old age.) Connecting the rooms, the hallways' dingy walls and vandalized murals can be downright depressing.

On the other hand, the lobby is a delight. Light pouring in through the arched windows shines on a dazzling tile floor and Victorian antiques. Massive square pillars, painted to look like white marble, help support a balcony of dark wood trimmed in gold. Also stunning is the Lithia Springs Restaurant. Decorated with long curtains and high-backed chairs, this intimate restaurant's crowning touch is an enormous 17th century crystal chandelier from Czechoslovakia. The food has an Italian bent, with lots of pasta and gourmet salads, and is a bit pricy ($15-20 for dinner), but then so is every other restaurant in Ashland.

The view from the mezzanine is delightful: a classy lobby decorated in brown and gold, with Victorian furniture and a patterned tile floor.

What to do in Ashland

For thirty years, Ashland's main attraction has been the **Oregon Shakespeare Festival**, just one block away from the hotel. Its classical and contemporary performances run from February to October and bring in millions of visitors each year. Ashland has become the cultural center of Southern Oregon, offering tourists a multitude of **fine restaurants, theaters**, and **music festivals**. In the town's main **plaza**, you can sample fresh lithia water from a drinking fountain (it tastes ghastly). To the west, lovely **Lithia Park** has forests, walking paths, and duck ponds. For more local history, look through the Southern Oregon Historical Society's museum in the turn-of-the-century **Chappell-Swedenburg House**.

Room Rates: Rooms $60-100, suites $100-105. Breakfast for two included. Cheaper rates available September-May.

Reservations: Three to six months in advance for summers and weekends.

Restrictions: Smoking and children okay.

Room Features: Private baths, telephones. Black-and-white TV sets may be requested.

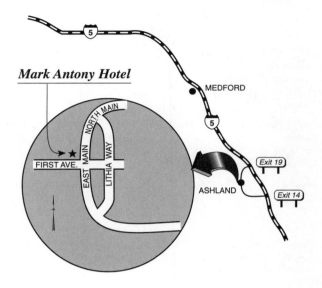

How to get there

From Interstate 5, take Exit 19 and go south on North Main Street. When this becomes East Main Street, start looking for the hotel on your right. It will be on the corner of East Main and First Avenue.

Further Reading

LOCAL TRAVEL

Brewster, David, and Irving, Stephanie. *Northwest Best Places.* Seattle: Sasquatch Books, 1993.

Fodor's Bed & Breakfasts, Country Inns, and Other Weekend Pleasures — The Pacific Northwest. New York: Fodor's Travel Publications, Inc., 1993.

Litman, Todd, and Kort, Suzanne. *Washington Off the Beaten Path.* Old Saybrook, CT: The Globe Pequot Press, 1993.

Logan, William Bryant, and Ochshorn, Susan. *The Smithsonian Guide to Historic America — The Pacific States.* New York: Stewart, Tabori & Chang, 1989.

Sakach, Tim & Deborah. *The Official Guide to American Historic Bed & Breakfast Inns and Guesthouses.* Dana Point, CA: Association of American Historic Inns and Guesthouses, 1987.

Simpson, Norman T. *Country Inns and Back Roads.* New York: Harper and Row, 1988-9.

Northwest Mileposts. Edmonds, WA: Alaska Northwest Publishing Co., 1988.

HISTORY

Cook, Jimmie Jean. *A Particular Friend, Penn's Cove.* Coupeville, WA: Island County Historical Society, 1973.

Evans, Lynette and Burley, George. *Roche Harbor — A Saga in the San Juans.* Everett, WA: B & E Enterprises, 1972.

Fricken, Robert E., and LeWarne, Charles P. *Washington: A Centennial History.* Seattle: University of Washington Press, 1988.

Griffin, Rachael, and Munro, Sarah, Ed. *Timberline Lodge.* Portland, OR: Friends of Timberline, 1978.

O'Donnell, Terence. *That Balance So Rare — The Story of Oregon.* Portland, OR: Oregon Historical Society Press, 1988.

"The Shelburne Hotel." *The Sou'wester.* Vol. XVI, No. 4. Winter 1981.

Shideler, John C. *Coal Towns in the Cascades.* Spokane, WA: Melior Publications, 1986.

Simpson, Peter. *City of Dreams — A Guide to Port Townsend.* Port Townsend, WA: Bay Press, 1986.

Snyder, Eugene E. *Portland Potpourri: Art, Fountains, and Old Friends.* Portland, OR: Binford & Mort Publishing, 1991.

"The Tokeland Hotel." *The Sou'wester.* Vol. V, No. 1. Spring 1970.

Webber, Bert and Margie. *Jacksonville, Oregon: The Making of a National Historic Landmark.* Fairfield, WA: Ye Galleon Press, 1982.

The majority of the information in this book comes from documents, magazines, newspapers, books, and personal interviews too numerous to be listed here.

Explore the West with UMBRELLA BOOKS ®

CALIFORNIA LIGHTHOUSES, a guide to the more than 40 lighthouse stations marking California's 1,200 miles of coast, by Sharlene & Ted Nelson. $12.95.

BICYCLING THE OREGON COAST, a bicyclist's discovery of the 370-mile route along America's most beautiful coastline, by Robin Cody. $10.95.

NORTHWEST NATURAL HOTSPRINGS, a guide that will make you want to jump into your car or boat and head for the nearest hotspring, by Tom Stockley. $10.95.

INLAND NORTHWEST ANTIQUE STORES, a humorous guide to the best antique stores of central and eastern Washington and north Idaho, by Bill London. $12.95.

INLAND EMPIRE (eastern Washington, northern Idaho), an introduction to many of the colorful residents and local lore in thirteen tours, by Bill London. $10.95.

WASHINGTON LIGHTHOUSES, the only guide available to Washington's 25 lighthouses, by Sharlene & Ted Nelson. $12.95.

PORTS OF CALL OF SOUTHEAST ALASKA, an insider's perspective on the region's independent people and unique places, by Sherry Simpson. $12.95.

ALASKA'S WILDERNESS HIGHWAY, a must companion for those planning to travel over the lonely, remote but beautiful Dalton Highway, by Mike Jensen. $10.95.

OREGON LIGHTHOUSES, a look at the legends associated with 14 lighthouses along the coast and up the Columbia River, by Sharlene & Ted Nelson. $10.95.

GRAND OLD HOTELS OF WASHINGTON & OREGON, an exploration to discover the finest of the region's historic hotels, inns, and lodges, by Christine Ummel. $12.95.

Mail your orders to: Epicenter Press, Box 82368, Kenmore Station, Seattle, WA 98028. Add $2 per book for book-rate shipping. (Washington residents must also add $.90 sales tax for each $10.95 title, $1.06 for each $12.95 title.)

KATRINA MILLER

About the Author

C hristine Ummel, 22, has lived in the Pacific Northwest since she was
    six years old. While growing up, she traveled widely through the
United States with her family, and learned to love far-away places. It was
on a later trip through Europe that she was surprised to develop a taste for
the quirkier aspects of history, and a passion for beautiful old buildings.

A recent honors graduate of Seattle Pacific University with degrees in
journalism and English literature, Christine is an associate editor and
publicity coordinator for Epicenter Press. She lives in the Seattle area.